Skills Assessments, Grad

Table of Contents

*PLEASE NOTE: Page 53 (Spelling) includes a list of 100 words that students should learn to spell. These are high-frequency words that are often misspelled. This list may be given to determine proficiency at the beginning of the year. A copy could be sent home for students to use as homework over an extended period of time.

Class Record Chart

Students	**Reading Overall**	Consonant Sounds	Short Vowel Sounds	Long Vowel Sounds	Vowel Sounds	Final Blends	Consonant Digraphs	Sight Vocabulary	Word Meaning	Word Meaning in Context	Words with Multiple Meanings	Antonyms	Synonyms	Classifying	Affixes and Compound Words	Details in a Story	Details in a Letter	Details in a Poem	Sequence	Main Idea	Conclusion	Studying the Story	Fantasy	Realistic Fiction	Nonfiction	**Language Arts Overall**	Capitalization and Punctuation	Nouns and Pronouns	Verbs	Word Order	Kinds of Sentences

Class Record Chart

Students	Spelling	Using Books	Title Page	Table of Contents	Alphabetical Order	Dictionary Skills	Paragraphs	Personal Narrative	Descriptive Paragraph	How-To Paragraph	Friendly Letter	**Math Overall**	Number Concepts	Addition	Subtraction	Addition and Subtraction	Geometry	Measurement	Patterns	Money	Time	Estimation	Charts and Graphs	Problem Solving: Whole Numbers	Problem Solving: Measurement and Geometry	Problem Solving: Time and Money	**Science Overall**	Earth and Space Science	Life Science	Physical Science	**Social Studies Overall**	Reading Maps	Using Time Lines and Charts

Name ____________________

Individual Student Chart

	Test	Retest
Reading Overall		
Consonant Sounds		
Short Vowel Sounds		
Long Vowel Sounds		
Vowel Sounds		
Final Blends		
Consonant Digraphs		
Sight Vocabulary		
Word Meaning		
Word Meaning in Context		
Words with Multiple Meanings		
Antonyms		
Synonyms		
Classifying		
Affixes and Compound Words		
Details in a Story		
Details in a Letter		
Details in a Poem		
Sequence		
Main Idea		
Conclusion		
Studying the Story		
Fantasy		
Realistic Fiction		
Nonfiction		
Language Arts Overall		
Capitalization and Punctuation		
Nouns and Pronouns		
Verbs		
Word Order		
Kinds of Sentences		
Spelling		

	Test	Retest
Using Books		
Title Page		
Table of Contents		
Alphabetical Order		
Dictionary Skills		
Paragraphs		
Personal Narrative		
Descriptive Paragraph		
How-To Paragraph		
Friendly Letter		
Math Overall		
Number Concepts		
Addition		
Subtraction		
Addition and Subtraction		
Geometry		
Measurement		
Patterns		
Money		
Time		
Estimation		
Charts and Graphs		
Problem Solving: Whole Numbers		
Problem Solving: Measurement and Geometry		
Problem Solving: Time and Money		
Science Overall		
Earth and Space Science		
Life Science		
Physical Science		
Social Studies Overall		
Reading Maps		
Using Time Lines and Charts		

Name ______________________ Date ____________

Reading Overall Assessment

Directions Say each picture name. Write the letter that stands for the missing sound.

a___

2. 

___eep

li___ard

Directions Darken the circle for the word that completes the sentence.

4. You can save money by putting it into a bank ____.

Ⓐ account Ⓑ equipment Ⓒ library

5. A window has the shape of a ____.

Ⓐ circle Ⓑ rectangle Ⓒ triangle

6. The ____ in most places is cold during the winter.

Ⓐ daylight Ⓑ post office Ⓒ weather

7. It is ____ to drink milk and eat healthy foods to keep teeth strong.

Ⓐ important Ⓑ polite Ⓒ decay

Directions Circle the words that answer the question.

8. Which are animals?

stork start short shark horse

horn bird lark sharp shirt

Name ________________________ Date ____________

Reading Overall Assessment, p. 2

Directions Darken the circle by the word that has the same or almost the same meaning as the underlined word.

1. My father is building a dollhouse for my sister.

Ⓐ asking
Ⓑ wanting
Ⓒ making
Ⓓ folding

2. When did you receive the package?

Ⓐ wrap
Ⓑ want
Ⓒ get
Ⓓ lose

Directions Read the story. Darken the circle for the correct answer.

Skippy

We have a new dog at our house. His name is Skippy. He is two years old. My sister and I like to play with Skippy. We throw a ball, and he brings it back. We take him for walks on our street. Skippy barks when he is hungry. I put food in his bowl. My sister gives him cool water. We take good care of Skippy.

3. How old is Skippy?

Ⓐ two months old
Ⓑ one year old
Ⓒ two years old
Ⓓ one week old

4. When does Skippy bark?

Ⓐ when he goes for a walk
Ⓑ when he wants food
Ⓒ when he wants water
Ⓓ when he is sad

5. Which of these is another good name for this story?

Ⓐ "How to Take Care of a Cat"
Ⓑ "Our New Pet"
Ⓒ "Fun with Dogs"
Ⓓ "Skippy and The Cat"

Name ______________________________ Date ______________

Consonant Sounds

Directions Say each picture name. Write the letters that stand for the missing sounds.

1.

___a___o___

2.

___ey

3.

boo___

4.

___ueen

5.

___at

6.

bu___

7.

___a___e___

8.

ro___ot

Name ______________________________ Date ______________

Consonant Sounds

Directions Say each picture name. Darken the circle next to the letter that stands for the missing sound. Write the letter to complete the word.

1.

○ p
○ t
○ b

mo___

2.

○ n
○ r
○ m

fa___

3.

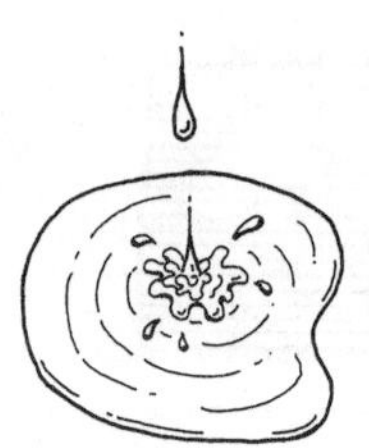

○ f
○ t
○ l

wa___er

4.

○ b
○ p
○ d

___og

5.

○ f
○ t
○ l

lea___

6.

○ g
○ c
○ s

___oat

7.

○ l
○ w
○ r

___ake

8.

○ h
○ t
○ l

sa___ad

Name ______________________ Date ______________

Short Vowel Sounds

Directions Say the vowel for the first picture in each row. Then, darken the circles under the pictures in the row that have the same short vowel sound as the first picture.

Name ______________________ Date ______________

Long Vowel Sounds

Directions Say the vowel for the first picture in each row. Then, darken the circles under the pictures that have the same long vowel sound as the first picture.

Name ______________________ Date ____________

Vowel Sounds

Directions Read each sentence. Darken the circle next to the word that completes the sentence.

1. The ____ like the corn.	Ⓐ birds Ⓑ barks Ⓒ burns
2. He grows ____.	Ⓐ churn Ⓑ curls Ⓒ corn
3. Mort lives on a ____.	Ⓐ fern Ⓑ farm Ⓒ far
4. Mort plants seeds in the ____.	Ⓐ dirt Ⓑ darn Ⓒ dart
5. Animals need a clean ____.	Ⓐ born Ⓑ barn Ⓒ burr
6. Mort has cows and ____.	Ⓐ hurts Ⓑ horns Ⓒ horses
7. At day's end, he rests on the ____.	Ⓐ porch Ⓑ part Ⓒ perk
8. Mort loads up his ____.	Ⓐ cord Ⓑ cart Ⓒ curl

Name ______________________ Date ______________

Final Blends

Directions Name each picture. Darken the circle of the correct picture name.

1. 

Ⓐ stump

Ⓑ stand

2. 

Ⓐ tent

Ⓑ test

3. 

Ⓐ plump

Ⓑ plant

4. 

Ⓐ desk

Ⓑ dust

5. 

Ⓐ wasp

Ⓑ wand

6. 

Ⓐ stamp

Ⓑ stand

7. 

Ⓐ jump

Ⓑ just

8. 

Ⓐ mask

Ⓑ nest

9. 

Ⓐ band

Ⓑ bump

10. 

Ⓐ dent

Ⓑ dusk

Name ______________________ Date ______________

Consonant Digraphs

Directions Name each picture. Darken the circle next to the missing letters. Write the letters.

1.

Ⓐ wr
Ⓑ kn
Ⓒ nk

___ock

2.

Ⓐ nk
Ⓑ ck
Ⓒ ng

si___

3.

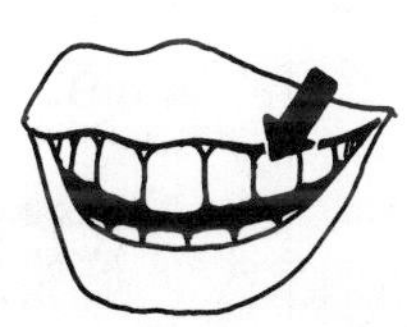

Ⓐ nk
Ⓑ ck
Ⓒ th

too___

4.

Ⓐ ch
Ⓑ ck
Ⓒ ng

clo___

5.

Ⓐ ck
Ⓑ th
Ⓒ ng

ki___

6.

Ⓐ th
Ⓑ ch
Ⓒ sh

fi___

7.

Ⓐ kn
Ⓑ ng
Ⓒ nk

___ee

8.

Ⓐ wr
Ⓑ ng
Ⓒ kn

___ite

Name ______________________ Date ______________

Sight Vocabulary

Directions Listen to the word that is called out. Darken the circle for the word that is called.*

1. Ⓐ after Ⓑ along Ⓒ also	**2.** Ⓐ few Ⓑ fine Ⓒ fly	**3.** Ⓐ goes Ⓑ good Ⓒ got	**4.** Ⓐ over Ⓑ on Ⓒ own
5. Ⓐ other Ⓑ part Ⓒ old	**6.** Ⓐ clean Ⓑ cost Ⓒ cold	**7.** Ⓐ place Ⓑ put Ⓒ part	**8.** Ⓐ ever Ⓑ each Ⓒ eat
9. Ⓐ grow Ⓑ gave Ⓒ goes	**10.** Ⓐ more Ⓑ made Ⓒ most	**11.** Ⓐ than Ⓑ that Ⓒ three	**12.** Ⓐ now Ⓑ small Ⓒ more
13. Ⓐ sleep Ⓑ seven Ⓒ stay	**14.** Ⓐ hold Ⓑ high Ⓒ help	**15.** Ⓐ cold Ⓑ kind Ⓒ know	**16.** Ⓐ she Ⓑ could Ⓒ should
17. Ⓐ saw Ⓑ sit Ⓒ six	**18.** Ⓐ yes Ⓑ say Ⓒ you	**19.** Ⓐ got Ⓑ grow Ⓒ get	**20.** Ⓐ eat Ⓑ eight Ⓒ enough
21. Ⓐ over Ⓑ enough Ⓒ end	**22.** Ⓐ where Ⓑ which Ⓒ when	**23.** Ⓐ can Ⓑ carry Ⓒ call	**24.** Ⓐ come Ⓑ cold Ⓒ carry

*Teacher note: For this assessment, the teacher may call out any of the three words in each block. Answers will vary accordingly.

Name ______________________ Date ______________

Word Meaning

Directions Read each meaning. Darken the circle for the word that best fits the meaning.

1. places of work

Ⓐ playgrounds
Ⓑ apartments
Ⓒ offices

2. to keep safe

Ⓐ protect
Ⓑ warning
Ⓒ chatters

3. name of a book

Ⓐ copyright
Ⓑ scalp
Ⓒ title

4. a machine that cuts

Ⓐ scissors
Ⓑ stethoscope
Ⓒ wheelbarrow

5. middle

Ⓐ short
Ⓑ final
Ⓒ center

6. person teaching a sport

Ⓐ audience
Ⓑ character
Ⓒ coach

7. people living around you

Ⓐ neighbors
Ⓑ listeners
Ⓒ catchers

8. hot season

Ⓐ winter
Ⓑ summer
Ⓒ autumn

9. pet doctor

Ⓐ veterinarian
Ⓑ x-ray
Ⓒ lizard

10. to see how big

Ⓐ measure
Ⓑ bloom
Ⓒ bud

Name ______________________ Date ______________

Word Meaning in Context

Directions Darken the circle for the word that best fits each sentence.

1. When the wind ___, the apples fell off the tree.

Ⓐ fell
Ⓑ rained
Ⓒ hopped
Ⓓ blew

2. A person who needs food to eat is ___.

Ⓐ thirsty
Ⓑ thirty
Ⓒ hungry
Ⓓ happy

3. People who travel on a bus are ___.

Ⓐ pilots
Ⓑ passengers
Ⓒ nurses
Ⓓ teachers

4. January is the first ___ of the year.

Ⓐ month
Ⓑ day
Ⓒ week
Ⓓ time

5. We ___ in the shallow end of the pool.

Ⓐ ate
Ⓑ studied
Ⓒ skated
Ⓓ swam

6. He was the best ___ on my baseball team.

Ⓐ singer
Ⓑ pilot
Ⓒ skater
Ⓓ batter

7. Pull the nails out with a ___.

Ⓐ bat
Ⓑ hammer
Ⓒ rope
Ⓓ stick

8. Birds use their bills to pick up ___.

Ⓐ pennies
Ⓑ meat
Ⓒ worms
Ⓓ potatoes

Name ________________________ Date ____________

Words with Multiple Meanings

Directions

Darken the circle for the word that fits both sentences.

1. Please ___ me that book.
What does the minute ___ on the clock say?

Ⓐ give
Ⓑ sell
Ⓒ find
Ⓓ hand

2. I'll plant a new flower ___ next spring.
My mother bought a new quilt for my ___.

Ⓐ row
Ⓑ chair
Ⓒ bed
Ⓓ watch

3. I will write a ___ to my grandmother.
I want to play that ___ on the piano.

Ⓐ letter
Ⓑ card
Ⓒ tune
Ⓓ note

Directions

Darken the circle for the sentence that is the correct answer.

4. Saul got a new back pack.
In which sentence does pack mean the same as in the sentence above?

Ⓐ The pack of dogs ran through the woods.
Ⓑ Be sure to pack my books.
Ⓒ I need a new pack of cards.
Ⓓ A tote bag is a kind of pack.

5. The river bank was very muddy.
In which sentence does bank mean the same as in the sentence above?

Ⓐ I lost my bank book.
Ⓑ My mother still has a piggy bank.
Ⓒ Let's walk along the bank.
Ⓓ Don't bank on me helping.

Name ____________________ Date __________

Antonyms

Directions Darken the circle by the word that has the opposite meaning of the underlined word.

1. Please shut the door.

Ⓐ close
Ⓑ fix
Ⓒ open
Ⓓ paint

2. She has thick hair.

Ⓐ straight
Ⓑ red
Ⓒ short
Ⓓ thin

3. After the movie, let's go to my house.

Ⓐ Sooner
Ⓑ Later
Ⓒ Before
Ⓓ Earlier

4. He has a damp swimsuit.

Ⓐ colorful
Ⓑ wet
Ⓒ dirty
Ⓓ dry

5. This magic trick always works.

Ⓐ often
Ⓑ never
Ⓒ soon
Ⓓ sometimes

6. Our teacher was absent yesterday.

Ⓐ away
Ⓑ present
Ⓒ returning
Ⓓ gone

7. She was too young to baby-sit.

Ⓐ weak
Ⓑ thin
Ⓒ old
Ⓓ small

8. The diving board is at the deep end of the pool.

Ⓐ well
Ⓑ wide
Ⓒ broad
Ⓓ shallow

Name ______________________ Date ______________

Synonyms

Directions Darken the circle by the word that has the same or almost the same meaning as the underlined word.

1. We had a visitor this afternoon.

- Ⓐ game
- Ⓑ guest
- Ⓒ cousin
- Ⓓ worker

2. Now he is finished.

- Ⓐ done
- Ⓑ gone
- Ⓒ here
- Ⓓ present

3. They want extra milk.

- Ⓐ less
- Ⓑ white
- Ⓒ ice
- Ⓓ more

4. Jean's dog is missing.

- Ⓐ sick
- Ⓑ lost
- Ⓒ young
- Ⓓ black

5. We heard a strange noise coming from the house.

- Ⓐ sound
- Ⓑ window
- Ⓒ smile
- Ⓓ story

6. Carol made that castle.

- Ⓐ bought
- Ⓑ saw
- Ⓒ built
- Ⓓ wanted

7. He's reading the front page.

- Ⓐ middle
- Ⓑ only
- Ⓒ first
- Ⓓ back

8. Can you hop on one foot?

- Ⓐ stand
- Ⓑ dance
- Ⓒ jump
- Ⓓ run

Name ______________________________ Date ______________

Classifying

Directions Circle the words that answer the question.

1. Which are things to ride?

van	jeep	keep
like	tan	bike

---

2. Which are things to eat?

run	meat	lake
cake	bun	seat

---

3. Which can you hear?

horn	harm	harp
chirp	part	purr

---

4. Which are on a farm?

barn	horse	corn
dirt	hard	herd

---

5. Which can you wear?

sport	shorts	star
shirt	fork	skirt

Name ______________________ Date ____________

Affixes and Compound Words

Directions

Darken the circle for the root word.

1. walking

Ⓐ ing
Ⓑ king
Ⓒ kin
Ⓓ walk

2. darkness

Ⓐ dark
Ⓑ ark
Ⓒ ness
Ⓓ dar

3. unhappy

Ⓐ un
Ⓑ hap
Ⓒ happy
Ⓓ appy

4. benches

Ⓐ ben
Ⓑ es
Ⓒ ches
Ⓓ bench

Directions

Darken the circle for the compound word.

5. Ⓐ department
Ⓑ address
Ⓒ sailboat
Ⓓ visit

6. Ⓐ remember
Ⓑ sunshine
Ⓒ over
Ⓓ away

7. Ⓐ buttercup
Ⓑ happiest
Ⓒ example
Ⓓ helpful

8. Ⓐ stamping
Ⓑ kinder
Ⓒ going
Ⓓ snowball

Name ______________________ Date ____________

Details in a Story

Directions Read the story. Darken the circle for the correct answer.

Did you know that owls are good hunters? Owls sleep all day long. At night they wake up and fly around. They look for mice to eat. Owls have very big eyes. Big eyes let in more light. Owls can see better at night than we can. Owls also hear very well. They can hear a mouse running in the grass. They can fly without making any noise at all. All these things make owls good hunters.

1. Which word tells how an owl can fly?

Ⓐ quietly
Ⓑ slowly
Ⓒ loudly
Ⓓ badly

2. This story does not tell ___.

Ⓐ why owls have big eyes
Ⓑ when owls wake up
Ⓒ about the different kinds of owls
Ⓓ what makes owls good hunters

3. When do owls sleep?

Ⓐ at night
Ⓑ during the afternoon
Ⓒ all day
Ⓓ never

4. What helps owls see at night?

Ⓐ their small eyes
Ⓑ their big eyes
Ⓒ streetlights
Ⓓ the Sun

5. How do owls hear?

Ⓐ well
Ⓑ poorly
Ⓒ never
Ⓓ only at night

Name ______________________ Date ____________

Details in a Letter

Directions Read the letter. Darken the circle for the correct answer.

Dear Wanda,

I haven't had one chance to write you for the past three months. I have been very busy in school. But now that school is over, I want to tell you what I have been doing.

I played on my school's softball team this spring. We won most of our games. Best of all, we traveled to different cities to play other teams. That was fun!

I have a big surprise for you. My mother gave me a new puppy for my birthday. My puppy is brown and black with a long tail and a white spot on her forehead. I named her Melissa. I can't wait for you to see her. When are you coming to visit this summer? Please write me soon.

Your cousin,
Alice

1. Melissa does not have ___.

- Ⓐ white feet
- Ⓑ brown feet
- Ⓒ a white spot
- Ⓓ a long tail

2. Alice and Wanda are ___.

- Ⓐ cousins
- Ⓑ best friends
- Ⓒ sisters
- Ⓓ teammates on the softball team

3. Alice's softball team ___.

- Ⓐ never lost a game
- Ⓑ won only four games
- Ⓒ won most of their games
- Ⓓ travels very little

4. What did Alice get for her birthday?

- Ⓐ a softball
- Ⓑ a puppy
- Ⓒ a new dress
- Ⓓ a kitten

Name ______________________ Date ____________

Details in a Poem

Directions Read the poem. Darken the circle for the correct answer.

The Acrobat

The cat tiptoes
across the back of the couch
like an acrobat
on a high wire.

With no net below
(in case of falls)
she holds her tail up—
a feather curling
toward the circus top,
and her whiskers out—
a pole for balance.

At the end
she hops quickly
onto the lamp table
as if that balancing act
had been a Sunday walk.

1. What does the cat use to keep her balance?

Ⓐ the lamp table
Ⓑ her whiskers
Ⓒ the back of the couch
Ⓓ a pole

2. What is another good name for this poem?

Ⓐ "A Falling Star"
Ⓑ "On a Sunday Walk"
Ⓒ "Circus Cat"
Ⓓ "Funny Clown"

3. The poem compares the cat to a ____.

Ⓐ circus performer
Ⓑ balancing pole
Ⓒ couch
Ⓓ feather

4. The phrase "a feather curling toward the circus top" describes the cat's ____.

Ⓐ whiskers
Ⓑ tail
Ⓒ walk
Ⓓ feet

Name ______________________ Date ____________

Sequence

Directions Read the paragraph. Think about the order in which things happen. Then, read the questions. Darken the circle in front of the best answer.

Right after lunch Juan gave his dog a bath. First, he got a big pail of water. Next, he got some soap. He got a big fluffy towel. Then, he got his dog, Dragon. Dragon liked his bath. He liked the fluffy towel. After his bath, Dragon dug in the dirt for his bone. Then, he ran to a mud puddle and rolled in it. It was fun for Dragon, but it was not fun for Juan. Dragon had to have another bath!

1. When did Juan give his dog a bath?

Ⓐ right after lunch
Ⓑ right after school
Ⓒ right after dinner

2. What did Juan do second?

Ⓐ He got a pail of water.
Ⓑ He got his dog.
Ⓒ He got some soap.

3. What happened after Dragon rolled in the mud puddle?

Ⓐ Dragon ate his dinner.
Ⓑ Dragon had another bath.
Ⓒ Dragon ran and played.

Name ______________________ Date ____________

Sequence, p. 2

Directions Read the paragraphs and answer the questions. Write your answers in complete sentences.

Jason had a fun day with his grandpa. First, they played catch with a ball. Then, they went to the park and flew Jason's kite. After that, Grandpa read a story to Jason, and then they both took a little nap.

1. What did they do after they played catch?

____

____

2. What did they do after Grandpa read the story?

____

Maria lost her doll. She looked all over for it. First, she looked under the bed. Then, she looked in her closet. After that, she looked on the chair. Finally, she found it in the buggy. Maria was happy to find her doll.

3. Where did Maria look first?

____

4. Where did she find her doll?

____

Name ______________________ Date ____________

Main Idea

Directions Read the story to yourself. Decide what the story is mainly about. Darken the circle in front of the correct answer.

William went many places after school. He needed a haircut, so he went to the barber shop. His mother needed some bread and milk, so he went to the store. He wanted to save the money his grandmother had given him, so he went to the bank.

1. What is the main idea of the story?

Ⓐ William got ten dollars from his grandmother.
Ⓑ William's mother needed milk and bread.
Ⓒ William went many places after school.

We played in the sand. We went swimming in the water. The sun felt nice and warm. We threw the beach ball to each other. We had a picnic at lunchtime. We had a fun day at the beach.

2. What is the story mainly about?

Ⓐ We had a picnic at lunchtime.
Ⓑ We had a fun day at the beach.
Ⓒ We played in the sand.

Name ______________________ Date ____________

Main Idea, p. 2

Directions Read each story. Think about the ideas in the story. Write the sentence that tells the main idea.

1. I saw a flag at my school. I saw another flag in the park. I saw three flags on a building by my house. The marchers were carrying flags in the parade down my street. I saw many flags in my neighborhood.

The main idea of the story is ______________________

____

2. Annie likes to play basketball. She likes to shoot baskets. She can throw the ball right through the net. Annie can bounce the ball very fast.

The main idea of the story is ______________________

____

3. Bill goes to the park with Jim. He plays basketball with Bobby and Julie. Bill likes to play games with Ben and Jason. He rides bikes with Maria and Mark. Bill has lots of friends. He even watches television with his friends.

The main idea of the story is ______________________

____

Name ______________________ Date ____________

Conclusion

Directions Read the stories to yourself. Then, answer the questions about what will happen next. Darken the circle in front of the correct answer.

Mrs. Cooper took the box of bread mix. She put it in a bowl. She added eggs, water, and some oil. She mixed it until it was smooth. Then, she put it in a pan.

1. What will happen next?

Ⓐ Mrs. Cooper will bake the bread in the oven.
Ⓑ Mrs. Cooper will eat baked eggs for lunch.
Ⓒ Mrs. Cooper will go for a walk.
Ⓓ Mrs. Cooper will bake cookies.

Annie filled the bathtub with water. She put her boats and toys in the water. She got her soap and her towel.

2. What will happen next?

Ⓐ Annie will ride her bike.
Ⓑ Annie will take a bath.
Ⓒ Annie will watch television.
Ⓓ Annie will leave for school.

Jason and his grandpa were getting ready. They got their worms. They got their hooks and lines. They went to the lake.

3. What will happen next?

Ⓐ Jason and his grandpa will swim.
Ⓑ Jason and his grandpa will fish.
Ⓒ Jason and his grandpa will eat lunch.
Ⓓ Jason and his grandpa will go home.

Name ______________________ Date ______________

Studying the Story

Directions Read the story. Then, answer the questions.

The Hole

One day, a small boy was walking down the street. Suddenly, he fell down a hole. It was a very deep, dark hole. The small boy couldn't see. He was really scared. What did he do? He fell asleep, of course!

A few hours later, the boy was awakened by singing. The voices were high-pitched and squeaky. Then, the boy saw hundreds of tiny candles.

They were being carried by hundreds of tiny mice. They led him to an underground elevator. The boy went up. He was back on the street!

1. What is the title?

____

2. Who are the characters?

____

3. What is the problem?

____

4. How is the problem solved?

____

____

Name ______________________ Date __________

Jared's Wish

Once upon a time, there lived a little boy named Jared. Jared lived with his grandmother in a small cottage in the woods.

Every morning, Jared went to the well to get water. His grandmother used five buckets of water a day. There was only one bucket, so Jared had to make five trips to the well each morning.

One day while Jared was at the well, he heard a little voice. "Help me!" he heard. Jared looked into the well and saw a tiny fairy splashing in the water. Jared reached down and lifted her out of the well.

"Thank you for saving me, little boy. For that I will give you one wish."

Jared thought for a few moments. "I would like to have a bucket big enough to carry all the water my grandmother needs in one day."

With that, the fairy sprinkled some dust on the bucket, and it grew five times bigger. Jared filled the bucket. He was a strong boy, so he had no trouble carrying it back to the cottage.

Go on to the next page.

Name ______________________ Date ______________

Jared's Wish, p. 2

Directions Answer each question about the story. Darken the circle for the correct answer.

1. How does the fairy thank Jared?

Ⓐ shakes hands with him
Ⓑ gives him money
Ⓒ gives him one wish
Ⓓ turns him into a man

2. How does the fairy help Jared?

Ⓐ She puts a spell on him.
Ⓑ She makes Jared's work easier.
Ⓒ She can fly.
Ⓓ She likes Jared.

3. How do you think Jared's grandmother feels about the bucket?

Ⓐ grateful
Ⓑ sad
Ⓒ angry
Ⓓ tired

4. How many trips does Jared have to make to the well each day?

Ⓐ one
Ⓑ three
Ⓒ five
Ⓓ ten

5. Why does Jared have to make so many trips to the well?

Ⓐ He has only one bucket.
Ⓑ He drinks a lot of water.
Ⓒ He wants to see the fairy.
Ⓓ He likes the daily chore.

Name ______________________ Date ____________

The Earthworm

Once upon a time, a young girl lived in a small house near a little stream. She lived alone, and no one knew about her troubles.

The girl had once made beautiful clothes of cotton that she grew and spun herself. She sold the clothes, so she was able to live well. But now the cotton would not grow. The soil seemed to be worn out. No matter what the girl did, the plants did not grow. With no money for food, the girl was thin and hungry. She did not know what to do.

Then one day, as she worked in her garden, she heard a tiny voice cry, "Help me! I'm stuck here on this wire, and I will surely die!" The girl looked around frantically. Finally, she found a little earthworm stuck on an old fence wire. She gently lifted the worm from the wire and set him on the ground. "Thank you so much," said the worm. "Your kindness will be rewarded."

"That's what everyone says," thought the girl. She returned to her work and went to bed that night cold and hungry.

The next morning, the girl walked hopelessly out to her garden. But what she saw was a surprise. Her cotton plants were healthier than they had ever been. Large balls of cotton burst from every plant. She ran to the garden and dropped to her knees. Then she noticed the worms. Thousands of earthworms had turned her sick, tired soil into the richest earth she had ever seen. She knew her troubles were over. "Oh, worm," the girl said. "Thank you so much." Both the girl and the worms lived happily ever after.

Go on to the next page.

Name ______________________ Date ____________

The Earthworm, p. 2

Directions Read each question. Answer each question in a complete sentence.

1. What was the cause of the girl's troubles?

____

____

2. What did the girl use the cotton for?

____

____

3. Where was the worm stuck?

____

____

4. Who lived happily ever after?

____

____

5. How did the worms help the girl?

____

____

____

Name ________________________________ Date ______________

Julio's Visit

Julio loves to visit his grandmother. He doesn't get to visit her very often because his family lives in a city that is six hours away. His grandmother lives in a big wooden house on a farm. It is old and looks like it has secret hiding places.

On the third Sunday of June, Julio's parents took him to his grandmother's. Since it was summer vacation, he was going to stay at Grandmother's for a whole month! His cousins Mario and Linda would soon be arriving. They would also be staying at their grandmother's this summer.

A big porch wraps around two sides of the house. Julio sat in the porch swing. He could see the trees that circle the house. They had been planted as a windbreak. They protect the house from the wind and blowing sand. The house is in the middle of a large, flat field. Julio watched the dirt road that leads to the house. He couldn't wait for his cousins to get there! Mario was Julio's age, and Linda was a year younger. They always had fun together. Last summer they had spent one whole morning making a fort out of sacks of seed that they found in the barn. Then Uncle Henry had taken them on a tractor ride.

Julio remembered another time with his cousins. They had gone out to explore the fields. Julio touched an electric fence and got a shock. Then they found an old snakeskin. Nothing like that ever happened at home!

Julio could smell the dinner that his mother and grandmother were cooking. He smelled ham, hot rolls, and pumpkin pie. It made him hungry.

Finally he saw a cloud of dust coming up the road. "They're here! They're here!" he shouted.

Go on to the next page.

Name ______________________ Date ____________

Julio's Visit, p. 2

Directions Darken the circle for the correct answer.

1. How do you think Julio felt when he saw his cousins arriving?

Ⓐ He was worried.
Ⓑ He was excited.
Ⓒ He was angry.
Ⓓ He was sad.

2. These boxes show things that happened in the story:

1	2	3
Julio went to his grandmother's house.		Julio thought about other summers at Grandmother's house.

What belongs in box 2?

Ⓐ Julio's cousins arrived at Grandmother's house.
Ⓑ Julio smelled dinner cooking.
Ⓒ Julio sat in the porch swing.
Ⓓ Julio saw a cloud of dust coming up the road.

3. What does <u>windbreak</u> mean in this story?

Ⓐ something that breaks easily in the wind
Ⓑ trees that protect a house from the wind
Ⓒ a big porch that wraps around a house
Ⓓ an old snakeskin

4. Julio's grandmother lives in a ____.

Ⓐ brick house
Ⓑ stone house
Ⓒ wooden house
Ⓓ new house

5. What do you think will happen next after Julio's cousins arrive?

Ⓐ They will build a fort on the hill.
Ⓑ They will look for snakeskins.
Ⓒ They will climb the trees in their grandmother's yard.
Ⓓ They will eat dinner at their grandmother's house.

Name ______________________ Date ____________

A Noise in the Attic

As we sat and ate dinner, I heard a funny sound from the attic. My parents did not even notice the sound, but I heard it and so did my little sister.

"What was that?" my sister asked.

"What was what?" my mother asked her.

"I heard it, too," I said.

Then it was quiet. I think the dog heard the sound because it ran under the chair.

"Dad," I said, "I need to get something from the attic. Can you help me?" I wanted to see the attic myself. I wanted to know what made the strange noise.

"We can go up there tomorrow, son," he said, but I knew that was too late.

After dinner, I decided to go into the attic myself. As I opened the door, I heard the sound again. It sounded like feet running across the floor. The door swung open and suddenly a gray, furry ball ran down the stairs and slid across the floor. It was a squirrel.

It took a while to get the squirrel out of the house. After we watched the squirrel run across the street, my dad said to me, "I'm surprised we didn't hear the squirrel in the attic."

Go on to the next page.

Name ______________________ Date __________

A Noise in the Attic, p. 2

Directions Read each question. Answer the question in a complete sentence.

1. How does the boy know there is something in the attic?

____

____

2. Why does the boy want to go to the attic?

____

____

3. Where did the dog hide?

____

____

4. What did the boy discover?

____

____

5. Where did the squirrel go at the end?

____

____

Name ______________________ Date ____________

Gravity

What helps you keep your feet on the ground? Gravity does! How does it do that?

Do you know what keeps us standing on Earth? Why don't we fall off? Why does everything we drop fall to the ground? Why do things feel heavy? It is all because of gravity. Many years ago, a scientist discovered gravity. His name was Isaac Newton.

Gravity is the pull that keeps things together. The larger a thing is, the more gravity it has. That is why we stay on Earth. It has a lot of pull. It pulls all objects toward it. That is why things feel heavy. The Earth is pulling everything we lift.

The Moon is not as large as the Earth. That is why astronauts who go to the Moon feel lighter. When they jump, they stay in the air longer. The Moon does not pull them back as strongly as the Earth does. The Moon does pull on the Earth's oceans. The gravity of the Moon causes the oceans to move back and forth. This is what makes high tides and low tides.

Gravity affects all things, from little ants to the planets around us. Gravity is an amazing force!

Go on to the next page.

Name ______________________ Date ____________

Gravity, p. 2

Directions Read each question about the story. Darken the circle for the correct answer.

1. Which is the main idea of the story?

Ⓐ Gravity is the force that keeps us on Earth.
Ⓑ The Moon pulls on the Earth's oceans.
Ⓒ Isaac Newton discovered gravity.

2. Because the Earth has gravity, ___.

Ⓐ people can float
Ⓑ objects fall when we drop them
Ⓒ the Moon is smaller than the Earth

3. Without the Moon, the oceans ___.

Ⓐ would have higher and lower tides
Ⓑ would have no fish
Ⓒ would not have tides

4. Who discovered gravity?

Ⓐ Thomas Edison
Ⓑ Isaac Newton
Ⓒ George Washington

5. Which sentence is true?

Ⓐ Gravity is the force that keeps things apart.
Ⓑ Gravity is the pull that keeps things together.
Ⓒ Gravity is the force that makes things move.

6. Which sentence is an opinion?

Ⓐ Gravity is very interesting.
Ⓑ The Earth has gravity.
Ⓒ The Moon has less gravity than the Earth.

Name ______________________________ Date ______________

More Trees, Please

Pine, oak, palm, and orange are all types of trees. They are all alike, but they are also different!

How are trees alike? All trees need sunlight, water, and soil to grow. The leaves use sunlight to make food for the tree. The roots take water from the soil. The water moves up the trunk to the branches. Twigs grow out from the branches, and leaves grow on the twigs. Bark covers and protects the tree.

How are trees different? Some grow tall and others stay short. Trees grow in many shapes. Their leaves are different, too. Trees grow in different kinds of weather. Palm trees grow in warm places. Pine trees grow in cool places. Some trees have fruit, like apples and oranges. Others have cones and nuts, like pine and oak trees.

Pine trees are green all year. They are evergreen trees. Their leaves are needles. Most evergreen trees have cones with seeds inside. Trees like maples and oaks have leaves that change color in the fall. They fall off before winter, and new leaves grow in spring. These are called deciduous (dē sij'o͞o əs) trees.

Trees are very important. They give us shade. Their roots hold the soil in place. They keep the air clean. They are homes for many animals. People use trees to make paper and other things. What would the Earth be like without trees?

Go on to the next page.

Name ______________________ Date ____________

More Trees, Please, p. 2

Directions Read each question. Answer each question in a complete sentence.

1. What do all trees need to grow?

____

____

2. What part of a tree takes water from the soil?

____

____

3. What do trees have for protection?

____

4. How do trees help people?

____

____

____

5. How does the water from the soil get to the leaves and branches?

____

____

Name ______________________ Date ____________

Language Arts Overall Assessment

Directions Darken the circle under the part of the sentence that needs a capital letter. If no capital letter is needed, darken the circle for None.

1. In may (A) | we are going (B) | on a trip. (C) | None (D)

2. I saw (A) | mr. Becker (B) | at the store. (C) | None (D)

3. my mother (A) | bakes the best (B) | chocolate cake. (C) | None (D)

4. Cheryl and lisa (A) | are learning (B) | to skate. (C) | None (D)

Directions Darken the circle next to the correct punctuation mark for each sentence.

5. I read a good book last week

Ⓐ ? Ⓑ . Ⓒ ,

6. Don't touch that knife

Ⓐ ? Ⓑ " Ⓒ !

7. Can you come to my house

Ⓐ . Ⓑ ? Ⓒ !

8. Will you play a game with me

Ⓐ . Ⓑ ? Ⓒ !

Name ______________________ Date ______________

Language Arts Overall Assessment, p. 2

Directions

Darken the circle for the correct answer. Use the Table of Contents to answer questions 1 and 2.

Table of Contents

1. On what page does Chapter 3 begin?

Ⓐ page 9 Ⓒ page 14
Ⓑ page 12 Ⓓ page 23

2. What is the title of Chapter 2?

Ⓐ Guppies
Ⓑ Types of Pets
Ⓒ If Your Pet Gets Sick
Ⓓ Picking the Right Pet

3. Which word is not spelled correctly?

Do you remembir (Ⓐ) when her cousin (Ⓑ) was here (Ⓒ)?

Directions

Darken the circle for the correct answer.

4. Which word is a noun?

She (Ⓐ) came (Ⓑ) to school (Ⓒ) early (Ⓓ).

5. Which word is a verb?

John (Ⓐ) hit (Ⓑ) the ball (Ⓒ) over the fence (Ⓓ).

6. Which word is a pronoun?

They (Ⓐ) don't (Ⓑ) play (Ⓒ) tennis (Ⓓ).

7. Which word comes first in alphabetical order?

Ⓐ body Ⓒ bloody
Ⓑ bone Ⓓ bore

8. Where should you look in a book if you want to know the author's name?

Ⓐ cover
Ⓑ the table of contents
Ⓒ the copyright page
Ⓓ title page

Name ______________________ Date ____________

Capitalization and Punctuation

Directions Read each sentence carefully. Darken the circle under the part of the sentence that needs a capital letter. If no capital letter is needed, darken the circle under None.

1.	We celebrate Ⓐ	three holidays Ⓑ	in november. Ⓒ	None Ⓓ
2.	Joyce's Aunt karen Ⓐ	bought her Ⓑ	a new scarf. Ⓒ	None Ⓓ
3.	My mother Ⓐ	and ms. Romano Ⓑ	are friends. Ⓒ	None Ⓓ
4.	Shana lives Ⓐ	on Lenox road Ⓑ	in Middletown. Ⓒ	None Ⓓ

Directions Darken the circle for the correct punctuation mark.

5. The lion is loose

Ⓐ ? Ⓑ " Ⓒ !

6. I met Lara at the library

Ⓐ ? Ⓑ " Ⓒ .

7. Do you know Mr. Chase

Ⓐ ? Ⓑ " Ⓒ !

8. Whose painting won first prize

Ⓐ . Ⓑ ? Ⓒ !

Name ______________________ Date ____________

Capitalization and Punctuation

Directions Darken the circle for the sentence with the **correct** periods, question marks, and commas.

1. Ⓐ Mr. J. Garcia was born on Oct 17 1965.
Ⓑ Mr J Garcia was born on Oct. 17 1965.
Ⓒ Mr. J. Garcia was born on Oct. 17, 1965.

2. Ⓐ Where was Dr. Blair on Apr. 12, 1989?
Ⓑ Where was Dr. Blair on Apr. 12, 1989.
Ⓒ Where was Dr Blair on Apr 12 1989?

3. Ⓐ Did you play on Dove St. last night.
Ⓑ Did you play on Dove St last night?
Ⓒ Did you play on Dove St. last night?

4. Ⓐ I will pack my clothes toys and books.
Ⓑ I will pack my clothes, toys, and books.
Ⓒ I will pack, my clothes, toys, and, books.

Directions Darken the circle for the sentence that has **correct** capitalization and punctuation.

5. Ⓐ Have you ever been to Orlando, Florida?
Ⓑ That's where disneyworld is.
Ⓒ Our family is going there
Ⓓ We're going in february.

6. Ⓐ Did you ever ride on a roller coaster.
Ⓑ My friend mark rode on one today.
Ⓒ He told me it was very scary.
Ⓓ He said i shouldn't ride it.

7. Ⓐ My friend hilary is moving.
Ⓑ She is moving to Erie.
Ⓒ We are both sad that she is moving
Ⓓ Next year i will visit her in her new house.

8. Ⓐ Wasn't that a good show,
Ⓑ My sister sari and I thought it was funny
Ⓒ My father liked it too?
Ⓓ My mother didn't see it.

Name ______________________ Date ______________

Nouns and Pronouns

Directions Read the sentences. Underline the nouns. Tell if each noun names a person, place, or thing.

1. Why is this house so funny? ______________
2. Alaska is beautiful. ______________
3. Watch out for the flying hat! ______________
4. That shoe is walking! ______________
5. Will the boy find it? ______________

Directions Read each sentence. Darken the circle for the pronoun that can take the place of the underlined noun.

6. <u>Tina's hamster</u> lives in a cage.

   Ⓐ They Ⓑ It Ⓒ She

7. <u>Tina</u> feeds her hamster every day.

   Ⓐ We Ⓑ It Ⓒ She

8. <u>James</u> has a hamster, too.

   Ⓐ We Ⓑ She Ⓒ He

9. <u>Tina and James</u> like to play with their hamsters.

   Ⓐ We Ⓑ They Ⓒ It

10. <u>My friend and I</u> went to visit Tina and James.

    Ⓐ We Ⓑ They Ⓒ It

Name ______________________ Date ______________

Verbs

Directions Darken the circle for the correct verb.

1. My baby sister ____ two years old.

Ⓐ be
Ⓑ are
Ⓒ is
Ⓓ am

2. We ____ a funny puppet show.

Ⓐ saw
Ⓑ seen
Ⓒ seed
Ⓓ have saw

3. Tamara ____ to the zoo.

Ⓐ went
Ⓑ going
Ⓒ goed
Ⓓ go

4. Did you see that bird ____ away?

Ⓐ flew
Ⓑ fly
Ⓒ flown
Ⓓ flewed

5. Dad ____ us to the beach.

Ⓐ taked
Ⓑ tooken
Ⓒ took
Ⓓ do take

6. They ____ under a shady tree.

Ⓐ sat
Ⓑ have sit
Ⓒ sitted
Ⓓ had sit

7. The boys ____ playing tag.

Ⓐ was
Ⓑ is
Ⓒ were
Ⓓ did

8. Where ____ they going?

Ⓐ is
Ⓑ was
Ⓒ have
Ⓓ are

Name ______________________ Date ____________

Word Order

Directions Read each sentence. Darken the circle by the sentence that is in correct word order.

1. Ⓐ Near the woods the house was.
Ⓑ The house near the woods was.
Ⓒ The woods near was the house.
Ⓓ The house was near the woods.

2. Ⓐ It was time home to go.
Ⓑ Home to go it was time.
Ⓒ It was time to go home.
Ⓓ To go home time it was.

3. Ⓐ Up and down the tree runned the squirrel.
Ⓑ The squirrel up and down the tree ran.
Ⓒ The tree up and down ran the squirrel.
Ⓓ The squirrel ran up and down the tree.

4. Ⓐ The car coming we did not hear.
Ⓑ We did not hear the car coming.
Ⓒ Hear the car coming we did not.
Ⓓ Coming the car we did not hear.

5. Ⓐ Don bought flowers for his mother.
Ⓑ Bought for his mother flowers did Don.
Ⓒ Flowers for his mother Don bought.
Ⓓ Bought flowers did Don for his mother.

6. Ⓐ Flowers in the spring bloom.
Ⓑ Bloom flowers in the spring.
Ⓒ Flowers bloom in the spring.
Ⓓ In the spring bloom flowers.

Name ______________________________ Date ______________

Kinds of Sentences

Directions Read the sentence. Darken the circle for the correct kind of sentence.

1. Sara read a story to her dolls.
Ⓐ statement Ⓑ question Ⓒ exclamation

2. Poor Ming fell asleep in her garden!
Ⓐ statement Ⓑ question Ⓒ exclamation

3. John was in his room.
Ⓐ statement Ⓑ question Ⓒ exclamation

4. Lisa works so hard!
Ⓐ statement Ⓑ question Ⓒ exclamation

5. Who came walking by?
Ⓐ statement Ⓑ question Ⓒ exclamation

6. The flowers started to grow.
Ⓐ statement Ⓑ question Ⓒ exclamation

7. What did Juan do?
Ⓐ statement Ⓑ question Ⓒ exclamation

8. Maria stopped to look at the birds.
Ⓐ statement Ⓑ question Ⓒ exclamation

9. What makes seeds grow?
Ⓐ statement Ⓑ question Ⓒ exclamation

10. Did Jose do anything else?
Ⓐ statement Ⓑ question Ⓒ exclamation

Name ______________________________ Date ______________

Spelling

Directions Darken the circle for the word that is spelled correctly.

1. We _____ go to the beach on hot days.

Ⓐ allways
Ⓑ always
Ⓒ alwayse
Ⓓ allwaze

2. Our new _____ is very nice.

Ⓐ nieghbor
Ⓑ naghbor
Ⓒ neighbor
Ⓓ neighber

3. The train will be at the _____ soon.

Ⓐ stashun
Ⓑ station
Ⓒ staytion
Ⓓ stashon

4. We are planning to bake _____ tomorrow.

Ⓐ bred
Ⓑ breed
Ⓒ brad
Ⓓ bread

5. Summer starts in _____.

Ⓐ Joon
Ⓑ June
Ⓒ Juin
Ⓓ Jiune

6. Vonnie's favorite color is _____.

Ⓐ perple
Ⓑ purpel
Ⓒ purple
Ⓓ purrple

7. Our class is going on a _____ at the beach.

Ⓐ picknic
Ⓑ picnic
Ⓒ picnick
Ⓓ picnec

8. My father took a _____ of the baby.

Ⓐ pichure
Ⓑ pickture
Ⓒ picteur
Ⓓ picture

Name ____________________ Date ____________

Spelling

Directions Darken the circle for the word that is not spelled correctly.

1. The fense will be painted early next week.
Ⓐ Ⓑ Ⓒ

2. Do you remembir when her cousin was here?
Ⓐ Ⓑ Ⓒ

3. The children were very qwuiet.
Ⓐ Ⓑ Ⓒ

4. That womin is my aunt's friend.
Ⓐ Ⓑ Ⓒ

5. Which do like better, cherryes or grapes?
Ⓐ Ⓑ Ⓒ

6. Evryone was invited to her party.
Ⓐ Ⓑ Ⓒ

7. I packed my best clotheing for our vacation.
Ⓐ Ⓑ Ⓒ

8. The baby is begining to crawl.
Ⓐ Ⓑ Ⓒ

9. That is the largest animel I have ever seen.
Ⓐ Ⓑ Ⓒ

10. We're haveing company for dinner tonight.
Ⓐ Ⓑ Ⓒ

Name ______________________________ Date ______________

Spelling

Directions Learn to spell these words. Use each word in a sentence. Spell these words correctly in all your writing.

about	didn't	instead	quarter	thought
address	different	judge	quit	through
again	distance	knew	quite	tired
all right	does	know	raise	tomorrow
along	early	laid	read	tonight
already	easy	letter	receive	train
always	enjoy	lever	remember	trouble
among	enough	little	right	truly
around	every	loose	rough	until
because	expect	loving	route	used
been	fierce	making	ruler	vacation
before	first	many	said	very
body	folk	maybe	says	wear
bought	forty	mother	school	weather
breathe	fourth	name	shoes	weigh
busy	friend	nice	since	were
buy	getting	none	sketch	we're
choose	goes	o'clock	skis	when
clear	group	off	solve	where
close	guard	often	some	which
come	guess	once	soon	white
complete	half	party	store	whole
could	haven't	past	straight	words
couldn't	having	peace	summer	would
count	hear	people	teacher	write
country	heard	played	tear	writer
dairy	here	plays	terrible	wrote
dear	hour	please	they	your
delete	house	pretty	they've	you're

Name ______________________ Date ______________

Using Books

Directions Darken the circle for the correct answer.

1. The name of a book is its _____.

Ⓐ contents
Ⓑ chapter
Ⓒ page
Ⓓ title

2. Where should you look if you want to know the parts and page numbers of a book?

Ⓐ the copyright page
Ⓑ the title page
Ⓒ the table of contents
Ⓓ the cover

3. If you want to know when a book was published, you should look on the _____.

Ⓐ cover
Ⓑ copyright page
Ⓒ title page
Ⓓ index

4. What is a place from which you can borrow books?

Ⓐ department store
Ⓑ library
Ⓒ hospital
Ⓓ supermarket

5. Where would you look to find how to spell a word?

Ⓐ math book
Ⓑ science book
Ⓒ dictionary
Ⓓ newspaper

6. A person who writes a book is called an _____.

Ⓐ author
Ⓑ editor
Ⓒ illustrator
Ⓓ actor

Name ______________________ Date ______________

Title Page

Directions Read the information in the box. It is from the title page of a book. Then, write your answers to the questions on the lines.

THE WORLD OF SHARKS by Deb Homan Photographs by Terry Green Whitewaters Press Florida

1. Where was it published? ______________________

2. What did Terry Green do for the book? ______________________

____

3. What is the title of the book? ______________________

____

4. Who wrote it? ______________________

Name ______________________ Date ____________

Table of Contents

Directions Look at the table of contents below. Then, read the questions. Darken the circle in front of the correct answer.

Table of Contents

1. What is on page 15?

Ⓐ The Sun
Ⓑ Watches
Ⓒ Wall Clocks
Ⓓ Early Clocks

2. Who wrote "Clocks Today"?

Ⓐ Timothy Watkins
Ⓑ Roland Mills
Ⓒ Betsy Roberts
Ⓓ Julio Mendez

3. What did Timothy Watkins write?

Ⓐ Clocks Today
Ⓑ Early Clocks
Ⓒ Wall Clocks
Ⓓ Telling Time

4. On what page could you find out about sundials?

Ⓐ page 8
Ⓑ page 14
Ⓒ page 17
Ⓓ page 5

Name ______________________________ Date ______________

Alphabetical Order

Directions Look at these names of different sports. The first letters are the same. Circle the word that would come first in each pair.

1. hockey
hiking

2. climbing
canoeing

3. football
flying

4. tubing
tennis

5. skiing
sliding

6. skating
swimming

Directions Look at each group of words. Put them in the correct alphabetical order. Write them on the lines.

7. barn ______________
basket ______________
baby ______________

8. hay ______________
hat ______________
happy ______________

9. cart ______________
cat ______________
call ______________

10. chicken ______________
chore ______________
chain ______________

Name ______________________ Date ______________

Dictionary Skills

Directions Choose the pair of guide words that you would use to find each word.

bat/boy	fit/fun	race/run	see/sit

1. room ______________
2. bath ______________
3. sent ______________
4. ranch ______________
5. flag ______________
6. sheep ______________

253

tiny/total

ti·ny very small.

toad a small animal that is like a frog.

to·day this day.

top·ic a subject in writing.

Directions Use the example dictionary page. Answer these questions.

7. What does today mean? ______________
8. What entry word means "very small"? ______________
9. Could the entry word tow be on this page? ______________
10. Which entry word comes second on the page? ______________
11. Which entry word tells about an animal? ______________
12. What are the guide words on this page? ______________

Name ______________________________ Date ______________

Paragraphs

Directions Read the paragraph. Answer the questions.

Saturday is the best day of the week for me. I can sleep later in the morning. I go shopping with my family. Sometimes, I ride my bike to my friend's house.

1. What sentence tells the main idea of this paragraph?

____

____

2. What is a detail that is in the paragraph?

____

____

Directions Write 1, 2, 3, or 4 to show what happened first, second, third, and last.

Eva planted flowers. First, she got a shovel. Next, she dug some holes in the garden. Then, she put the flowers into the holes. Last, she put the shovel back in its place.

3. ____________ Then, she put the flowers into the holes.

____________ Next, she dug some holes in the garden.

____________ Last, she put the shovel back in its place.

____________ First, she got a shovel.

Name ______________________________ Date ______________

Personal Narrative

Directions Read the story. Answer the questions.

My family and I love holidays. We think Thanksgiving is the best. All my grandparents come to our house. First, we sit at a very long table. Then, my sister brings in the food. The turkey always smells great! It tastes even better. After dinner we sing songs. We have a good time. Last of all, we hug each other good-bye. I can't wait for the next holiday!

1. Write three words from the story that show it is a personal narrative. ______________________________

2. Write a word from the story that tells the order in which things happen. ______________________________

3. Write a sentence about your favorite holiday. ______________________________

____

____

____

Name ________________________________ Date ______________

Descriptive Paragraph

Directions Read the paragraph. Then, answer the questions.

I just love a parade. I like to see the band march by. The uniforms shine with brass buttons and gold braid. The loud music always makes me want to clap my hands. I also like to see the floats. The floats with storybook characters are the best.

1. What is the topic of the paragraph?

____

2. Which sentence describes the band?

____

____

____

3. Write a sentence to add to the paragraph.

____

____

4. What word describes the music? ____________________

Name ______________________________ Date ______________

How-To Paragraph

Directions Read the paragraph. Then, answer the questions.

Sewing on a button can be easy. First, get a needle and thread. You will also need the button and a piece of clothing. Choose a thread color to match the clothing. Next, thread the needle. Then, sew on the button tightly. Last, make a knot in the thread. Cut the thread.

1. What is the topic sentence?

____

____

2. What is the first step?

____

3. What things do you need to sew on a button?

____

____

4. What would be a good topic for a how-to paragraph?

____

Name ______________________________ Date ______________

Friendly Letter

Directions Read the letter. Then, answer the questions about it.

> October 22, 2000
>
> Dear Grandma,
>
> The sweater you knitted for my birthday is great! The fall days here have been chilly. It's nice to have a new warm sweater to wear. It is just the right size. Thank you, Grandma.
>
> Love,
> Emily

1. Why did Emily write the letter?

____

____

____

2. To whom did Emily write the letter?

____

3. When did Emily write the letter?

____

4. What did Emily write that Grandma might like to know?

____

Name ______________________ Date ____________

Math Overall Assessment

Directions Darken the circle for the correct answer.

1. What is the difference?

$$\begin{array}{r} 31 \\ -\ 4 \\ \hline \end{array}$$

Ⓐ 37 Ⓒ 17
Ⓑ 25 Ⓓ 27

2. Which is the greatest amount?

Ⓐ twelve Ⓒ 11
Ⓑ 10 + 6 Ⓓ 1 ten 4 ones

3. Which is another way to write $1\frac{1}{2}$ hours?

Ⓐ sixty minutes
Ⓑ ninety minutes
Ⓒ thirty minutes
Ⓓ forty minutes

4. Which figure fits next in this pattern?

□ △ □ ○ □ △ ?

Ⓐ △
Ⓑ ○
Ⓒ □

5. Which number is eighty-nine?

Ⓐ 809 Ⓒ 98
Ⓑ 89 Ⓓ 908

6. Which is the sum?

$$\begin{array}{r} 12 \\ +\ 7 \\ \hline \end{array}$$

Ⓐ 20 Ⓒ 19
Ⓑ 15 Ⓓ 5

7. What amount is shown?

Ⓐ 52 cents

Ⓑ 42 cents

Ⓒ 47 cents

8. Round 17 to the nearest 10.

Ⓐ 10 Ⓒ 20
Ⓑ 15 Ⓓ 30

9. What is the perimeter of this rectangle?

Ⓐ 5 feet

Ⓑ 6 feet
Ⓒ 10 feet
Ⓓ 12 feet

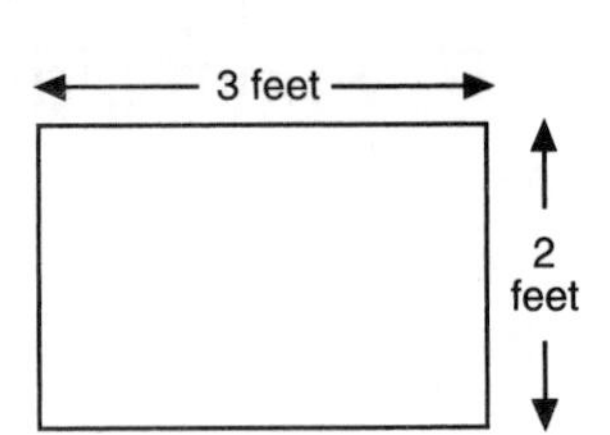

10. Which number will make both of these sentences true?

□ + 5 = 14
14 − □ = 5

Ⓐ 6 Ⓒ 8
Ⓑ 7 Ⓓ 9

Name ______________________ Date ______________

Math Overall Assessment, p. 2

Directions Write the number that the blocks show.

1.

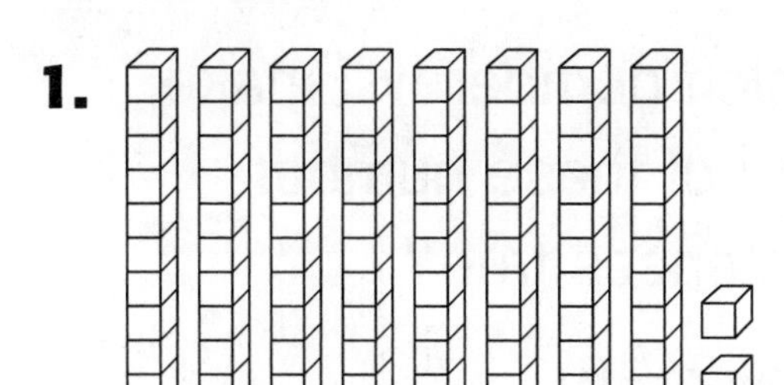

____

2.

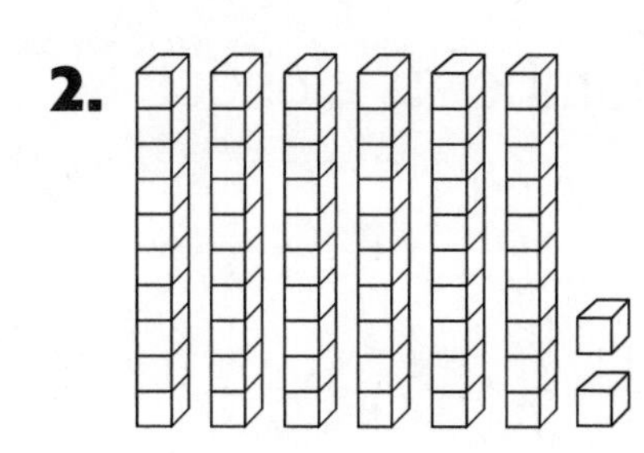

____

3. 5 tens and 9 ones ______________

4. 8 tens and 6 ones ______________

Directions Write < or > in each circle.

5. 56 ◯ 54 **6.** 36 ◯ 37 **7.** 35 ◯ 52

Directions Solve and write the answer.

8. $\begin{array}{r} 27 \\ +\ 38 \\ \hline \end{array}$

9. $\begin{array}{r} 56 \\ +\ 43 \\ \hline \end{array}$

10. $\begin{array}{r} 87 \\ -\ 58 \\ \hline \end{array}$

Directions Write the times.

11.

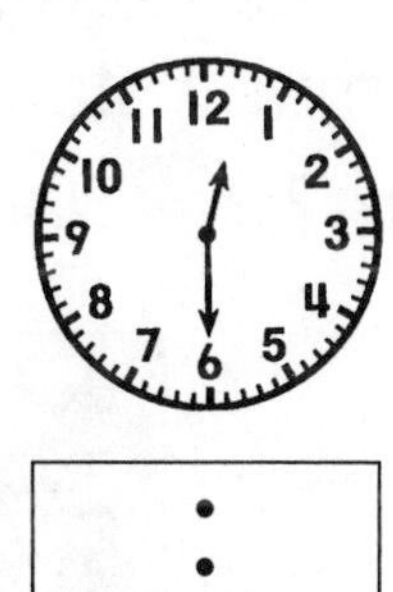

:

12.

:

13.

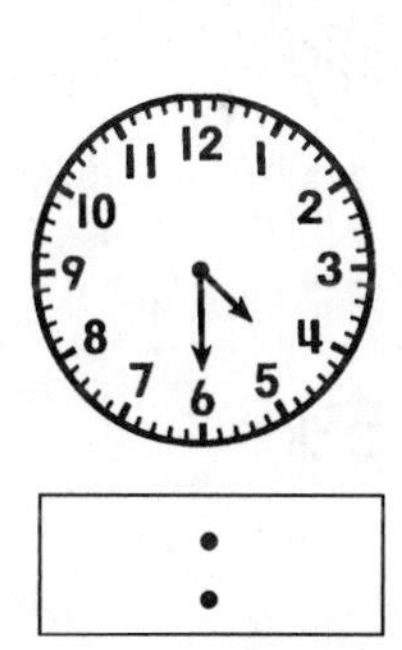

:

Directions Write the number that comes before or after.

14. ________, 694 **15.** ________, 377 **16.** 709, ________

Name ______________________ Date ______________

Number Concepts

Directions Darken the circle for the correct answer.

1. Which number is closest to 80?

- Ⓐ 75
- Ⓑ 83
- Ⓒ 85
- Ⓓ 90

2. Which number sentence does not equal 17?

- Ⓐ 9 + 8
- Ⓑ 20 – 3
- Ⓒ 10 + 7
- Ⓓ 17 – 1

3. Which number in the box is the second highest?

77	79	59	51

- Ⓐ 51
- Ⓑ 79
- Ⓒ 77
- Ⓓ 59

4. Which number will make both of these number sentences true?

17 – ? = 8

8 + ? = 17

- Ⓐ 10
- Ⓑ 7
- Ⓒ 9
- Ⓓ 6

5. Which number shows how many blocks there are?

- Ⓐ 30
- Ⓑ 34
- Ⓒ 22
- Ⓓ 24

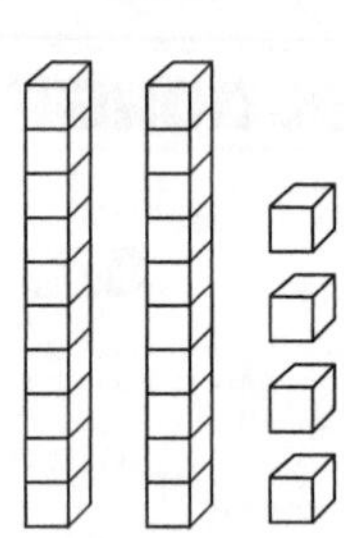

6. Which number sentence shows how many stars are in this picture?

- Ⓐ 3×5
- Ⓑ $3 + 5$
- Ⓒ $5 + 15$
- Ⓓ $3 + 3 + 5$

Name ______________________ Date ______________

Number Concepts

Directions Darken the circle for the correct answer.

1. In which place in the line is the girl?

Ⓐ first
Ⓑ second
Ⓒ third
Ⓓ fourth

2. Which group of numbers shows counting by 3s?

Ⓐ 11, 12, 13
Ⓑ 3, 6, 9
Ⓒ 13, 15, 17
Ⓓ 10, 12, 14

3. Which is an even number that is in the circle but not in the square?

Ⓐ 11
Ⓑ 12
Ⓒ 14
Ⓓ 13

11 13 12
16 14 15

4. Which number is greater than the other numbers?

Ⓐ $5 + 9$
Ⓑ 1 ten and 3 ones
Ⓒ sixteen
Ⓓ 12

5. Which sign is missing in this number sentence?

$6 \ ? \ 3 = 9$

Ⓐ $-$
Ⓑ $\times$
Ⓒ $+$
Ⓓ $<$

6. Which number has a 4 in the ones place?

Ⓐ 43
Ⓑ 124
Ⓒ 142
Ⓓ 410

Name ______________________ Date ____________

Addition

Directions Darken the circle for the correct answer.

1. 127
+ 38

Ⓐ 165
Ⓑ 155
Ⓒ 156
Ⓓ 158

2. 48
15
+ 27

Ⓐ 88
Ⓑ 90
Ⓒ 80
Ⓓ 70

3. 18 + 5 =

Ⓐ 9
Ⓑ 22
Ⓒ 23
Ⓓ 13

4. 34
+ 32

Ⓐ 56
Ⓑ 62
Ⓒ 66
Ⓓ 67

5. 4 + 6 + 9 =

Ⓐ 10
Ⓑ 18
Ⓒ 19
Ⓓ 17

6. 21
45
+ 14

Ⓐ 79
Ⓑ 80
Ⓒ 89
Ⓓ 70

7. 50 + 30 =

Ⓐ 53
Ⓑ 80
Ⓒ 530
Ⓓ 70

8. 20
+ 5

Ⓐ 35
Ⓑ 37
Ⓒ 25
Ⓓ 15

Name ______________________ Date ______________

Subtraction

Directions Darken the circle for the correct answer.

1. 50 – 20 =

Ⓐ 3
Ⓑ 30
Ⓒ 13
Ⓓ 40

2. $\begin{array}{r} 66 \\ -\ 27 \\ \hline \end{array}$

Ⓐ 29
Ⓑ 39
Ⓒ 41
Ⓓ 49

3. 51 – 5 =

Ⓐ 1
Ⓑ 44
Ⓒ 46
Ⓓ 47

4. $\begin{array}{r} 11 \\ -\ 4 \\ \hline \end{array}$

Ⓐ 15
Ⓑ 13
Ⓒ 7
Ⓓ 8

5. $\begin{array}{r} 36 \\ -\ 14 \\ \hline \end{array}$

Ⓐ 22
Ⓑ 23
Ⓒ 20
Ⓓ 12

6. $\begin{array}{r} 92 \\ -\ 41 \\ \hline \end{array}$

Ⓐ 41
Ⓑ 51
Ⓒ 42
Ⓓ 61

7. 18 – 9 =

Ⓐ 7
Ⓑ 8
Ⓒ 9
Ⓓ 6

8. 13 – 10 =

Ⓐ 10
Ⓑ 7
Ⓒ 3
Ⓓ 5

Name ______________________ Date ______________

Addition and Subtraction

Directions Solve.

1. $\begin{array}{r} 9 \\ +\ 9 \\ \hline \end{array}$

2. $\begin{array}{r} 11 \\ -\ 4 \\ \hline \end{array}$

3. $\begin{array}{r} 32 \\ -\ 9 \\ \hline \end{array}$

4. $\begin{array}{r} 15 \\ -\ 7 \\ \hline \end{array}$

5. $\begin{array}{r} 12 \\ -\ 4 \\ \hline \end{array}$

6. $\begin{array}{r} 54 \\ -\ 41 \\ \hline \end{array}$

7. $\begin{array}{r} 65 \\ +\ 9 \\ \hline \end{array}$

8. $\begin{array}{r} 24 \\ +\ 27 \\ \hline \end{array}$

9. $\begin{array}{r} 27 \\ +\ 38 \\ \hline \end{array}$

10. $\begin{array}{r} 50 \\ -\ 16 \\ \hline \end{array}$

11. $\begin{array}{r} 18 \\ +\ 66 \\ \hline \end{array}$

12. $\begin{array}{r} 36 \\ +\ 35 \\ \hline \end{array}$

Name ______________________ Date ______________

Geometry

Directions Darken the circle by the correct answer to each problem.

1. How many triangles are in the bag?

Ⓐ 3
Ⓑ 5
Ⓒ 2
Ⓓ 4

2. Which of these can be folded on the dotted line so both sides will match?

Ⓐ A
Ⓑ B
Ⓒ C
Ⓓ D

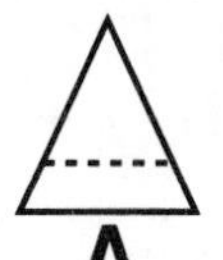
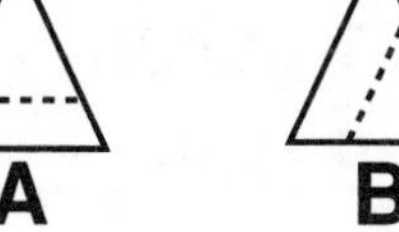
A B

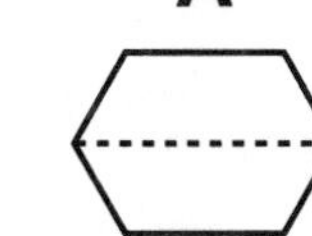
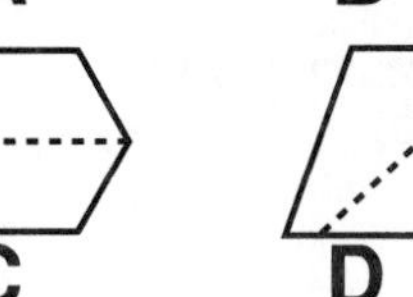
C D

3. What number is inside both the square and the circle?

Ⓐ 2
Ⓑ 3
Ⓒ 9
Ⓓ 10

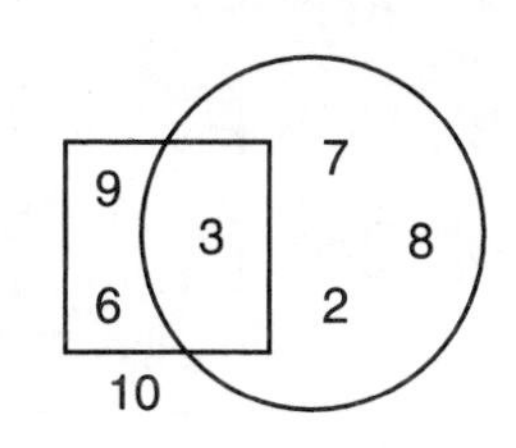

4. Which of these shapes is a cylinder?

A B C D

Ⓐ A
Ⓑ B
Ⓒ C
Ⓓ D

5. Which shape has 4 triangles in it?

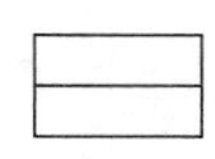
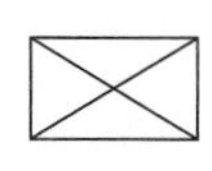
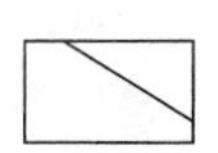
A B C D

Ⓐ A
Ⓑ B
Ⓒ C
Ⓓ D

6. How many sides are in this figure?

Ⓐ 6
Ⓑ 8
Ⓒ 10
Ⓓ 5

7. Which number inside the square and triangle is an odd number?

Ⓐ 2
Ⓑ 9
Ⓒ 7
Ⓓ 3

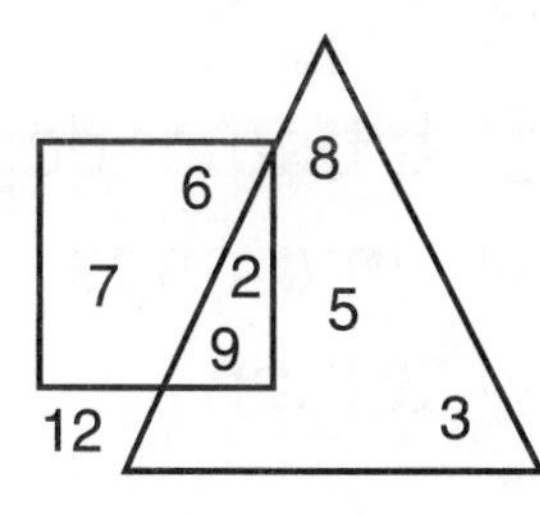

8. Which figure has a triangle inside a circle?

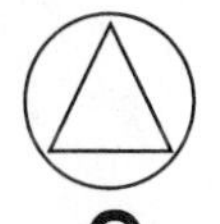
A B C

Ⓐ A
Ⓑ B
Ⓒ C
Ⓓ None of these

Name ______________________ Date ______________

Measurement

Directions Darken the circle for the correct answer.

1. How many leaves long is the rake?

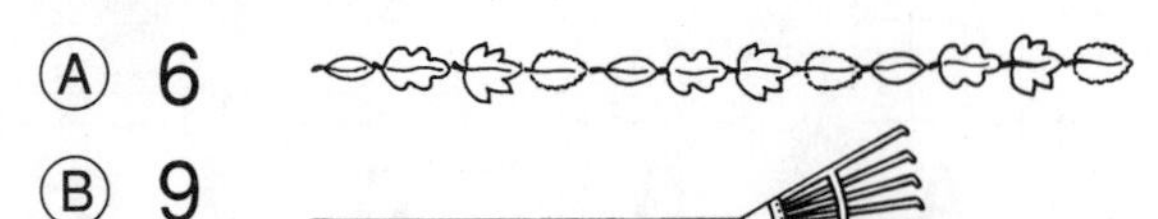

Ⓐ 6
Ⓑ 9
Ⓒ 12
Ⓓ 14

2. Which of these would be the weight of an apple?

Ⓐ 32 ounces
Ⓑ 16 ounces
Ⓒ 4 ounces

3. Which of these would weigh 5 kilograms?

Ⓐ a bag of dog food
Ⓑ an orange
Ⓒ a man

4. A glass of juice is most likely _____.

Ⓐ 1 cup
Ⓑ 1 quart
Ⓒ 1 gallon

5. How many degrees does this thermometer show?

Ⓐ 60
Ⓑ 51
Ⓒ 55
Ⓓ 54

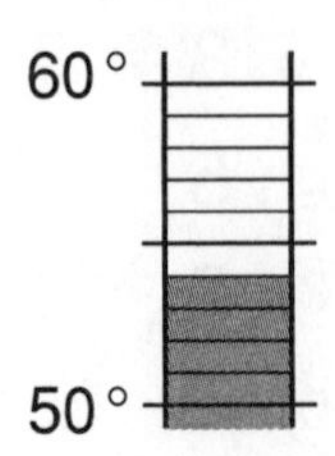

6. Four quarts is the same as _____.

Ⓐ 1 gallon
Ⓑ 2 pints
Ⓒ 8 cups

7. What temperature would be best for swimming outside?

Ⓐ 40° F
Ⓑ 80° F
Ⓒ 25° F

8. How much would a pumpkin weigh?

Ⓐ 6 tons
Ⓑ 6 ounces
Ⓒ 6 pounds

Name ______________________ Date ____________

Patterns

Directions Write the answers for questions 1 and 2.

88	75	93	85	89

1. Write the numbers from the greatest to the least.

________, ________, ________, ________, ________

2. Count back by 3's. Write the missing numbers.

34, ________, ________, ________, 22, ________,

________, 13, ________, ________, ________, 1

Directions Darken the circle for the correct answer.

3. Which number fits next in the pattern?

50, 75, 100, 125, _____

Ⓐ 175
Ⓑ 150
Ⓒ 135
Ⓓ 165

4. Which figure is missing in this pattern?

Ⓐ star
Ⓑ circle
Ⓒ triangle
Ⓓ square

5. Which group of numbers is missing from the pattern?

8, 10, 12, _____, _____, _____, 20

Ⓐ 13, 14, 15
Ⓑ 2, 4, 6
Ⓒ 14, 16, 18
Ⓓ 22, 24, 26

6. Which number belongs in the space?

45, 50, _____, 60, 65

Ⓐ 40 Ⓒ 70
Ⓑ 35 Ⓓ 55

Name ______________________ Date ______________

Money

Directions Count on to find the total amount. Then, write it in the box.

1.     

_____ ¢ _____ ¢ _____ ¢ _____ ¢ _____ ¢ [ ] ¢

2.  

_____ ¢ _____ ¢ [ ] ¢

3.  

_____ ¢ _____ ¢ [ ] ¢

4.      

_____ ¢ _____ ¢ _____ ¢ _____ ¢ _____ ¢ _____ ¢ [ ] ¢

Directions Darken the circle for the correct amount.

5.       

46¢	**60¢**	**37¢**	**42¢**
Ⓐ	Ⓑ	Ⓒ	Ⓓ

6.  

31¢	**16¢**	**36¢**	**61¢**
Ⓐ	Ⓑ	Ⓒ	Ⓓ

Name ______________________ Date ______________

Time

Directions Write the times.

1.

2.

3.

4.

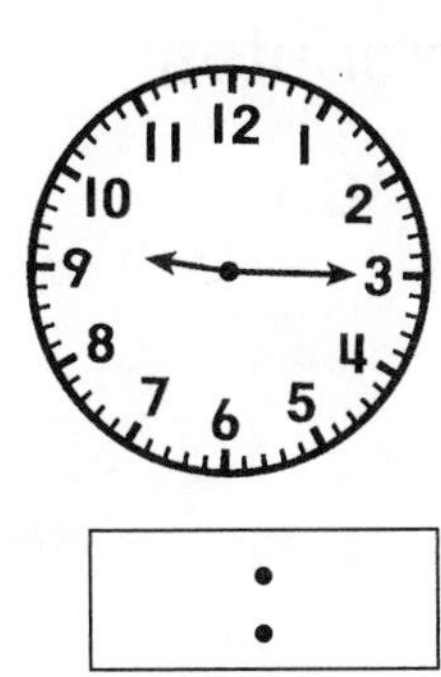

5.

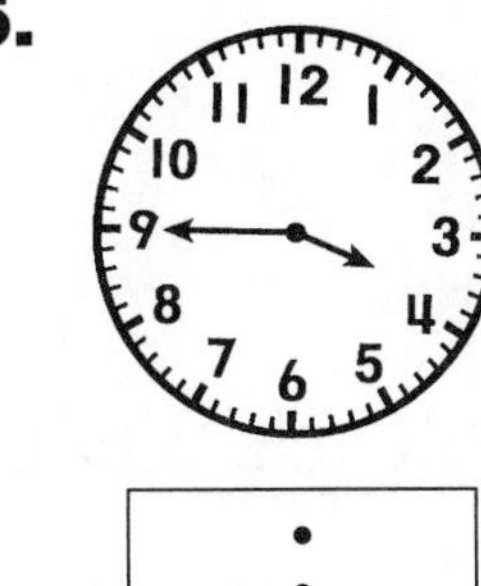

6.

Directions Darken the circle for the correct answer.

7. What time is it 15 minutes after 2:00?

Ⓐ 2:30
Ⓑ 2:15
Ⓒ 3:00

8. What time is it 4 hours after 10:30?

Ⓐ 3:00
Ⓑ 3:30
Ⓒ 2:30

9. Which is the time on the digital clock?

3:30

Ⓐ 3 o'clock
Ⓑ 30 minutes after 3
Ⓒ 15 minutes after 3

10. Which one of these shows the time on the round clock?

Ⓐ 5:00
Ⓑ 8:00
Ⓒ 3:00

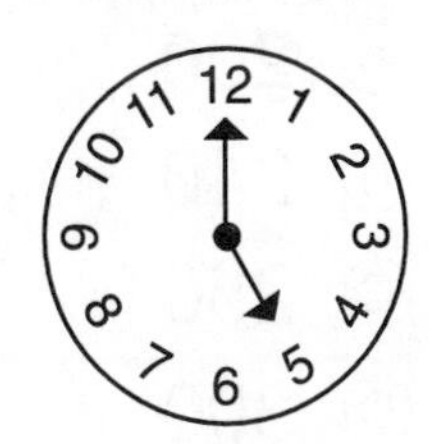

Name ______________________ Date ____________

Estimation

Directions Circle how much time each activity takes.

1. hearing a story

more than 1 hour

about 10 minutes

about 1 hour

2. one lesson at school

more than 1 hour

about 10 minutes

about 1 hour

Directions Look at each shape. Circle your estimate.

3.

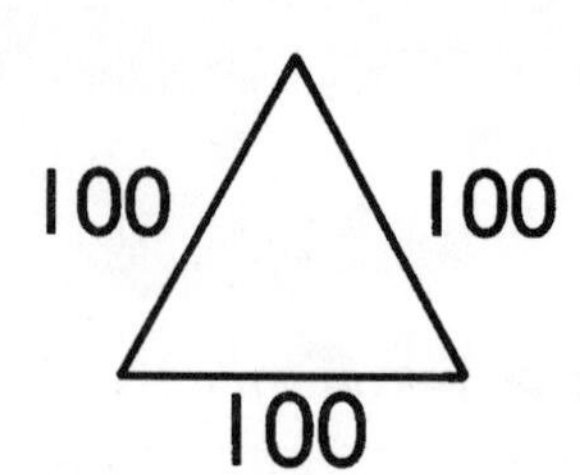

The perimeter is

< 400 $\qquad$ > 400.

4.

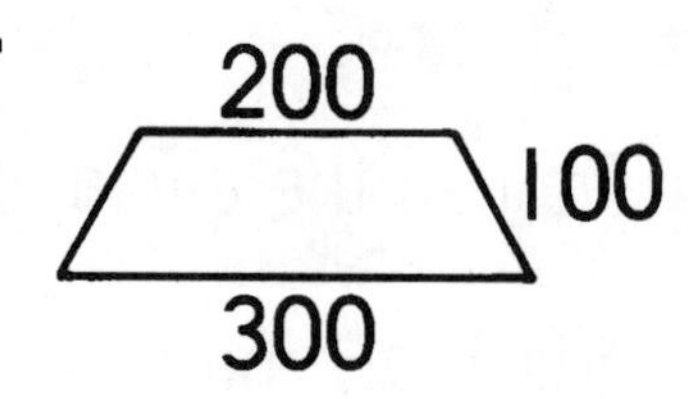

The perimeter is

< 500 $\qquad$ > 500.

Directions Darken the circle for the correct answer.

5. Round 245 to the nearest 100.

Ⓐ 200

Ⓑ 240

Ⓒ 250

Ⓓ 300

6. Round 35 to the nearest 10.

Ⓐ 30

Ⓑ 35

Ⓒ 40

Ⓓ 50

Name ______________________________ Date ______________

Charts and Graphs

Directions

Use the chart to answer questions 1–3. Darken the circle for the correct answer.

	Kareem	Delia	Ling	Stacy
Game 1	𝍸 //	//	𝍸	/
Game 2	𝍸	𝍸	𝍸	𝍸
Game 3	𝍸 𝍸	𝍸	/	///

1. Which student had a total of 22 points in all 3 games?

Ⓐ Kareem
Ⓑ Delia
Ⓒ Stacy
Ⓓ Ling

2. Who scored the fewest points in game 3?

Ⓐ Stacy
Ⓑ Ling
Ⓒ Kareem
Ⓓ Delia

3. Who scored the second most points?

Ⓐ Kareem
Ⓑ Ling
Ⓒ Delia
Ⓓ Stacy

Directions

Use the bar graph to answer questions 4–6. Darken the circle for the correct answer.

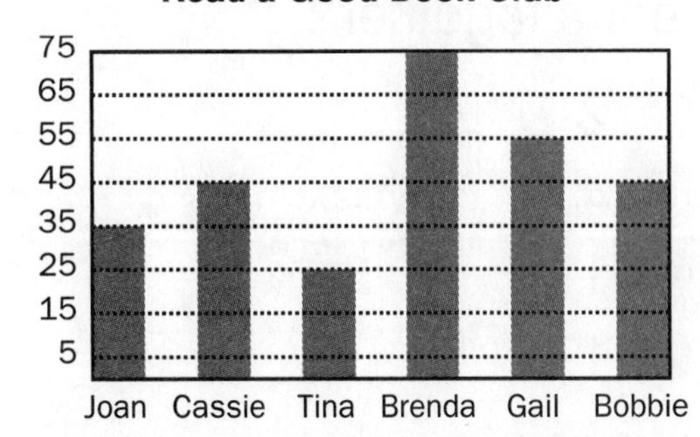

4. How many more books did Gail read than Bobbie read?

Ⓐ 5
Ⓑ 10
Ⓒ 15
Ⓓ 20

5. Who read the most books?

Ⓐ Cassie
Ⓑ Joan
Ⓒ Brenda
Ⓓ Gail

6. How many books did Tina read?

Ⓐ 35
Ⓑ 25
Ⓒ 40
Ⓓ 45

Name ______________________ Date ____________

Problem Solving: Whole Numbers

Directions Darken the circle for the correct answer.

1. Andy ate 7 pretzels. Luis ate 5 pretzels. How many pretzels did Andy and Luis eat altogether?

Ⓐ 2
Ⓑ 4
Ⓒ 11
Ⓓ 12

7 5

2. Tish had 14 toy turtles. She gave 8 turtles to her friends. How many turtles did Tish have left?

Ⓐ 22
Ⓑ 9
Ⓒ 6
Ⓓ 4

3. Janet is 5 years younger than Manuel. Manuel is 3 years younger than Jack. Jack is 13. How old is Janet?

Ⓐ 16
Ⓑ 11
Ⓒ 5
Ⓓ 8

4. If there are 3 girls, 2 boys, and 1 adult on a bus, how many people are on the bus?

Ⓐ 5
Ⓑ 7
Ⓒ 6
Ⓓ 8

5. If you have 3 blue pens, 3 red pens, and 1 black pen, how many pens do you have in all?

Ⓐ 5
Ⓑ 7
Ⓒ 6
Ⓓ 4

6. If you take 4 marbles from this bag, how many will be left?

Ⓐ 6
Ⓑ 4
Ⓒ 10
Ⓓ 8

Name ______________________ Date ____________

Problem Solving: Measurement and Geometry

Directions Darken the circle for the correct answer.

1. Tina's book is 9 inches long. It is 6 inches wide. What is the perimeter of Tina's book?

Ⓐ 30 inches Ⓑ 18 inches Ⓒ 15 inches

2. John has 3 pencils. Each pencil is 8 centimeters long. He has his pencils in the shape of a triangle. What is the perimeter of the triangle?

Ⓐ 8 centimeters Ⓑ 32 centimeters Ⓒ 24 centimeters

3. Diego's room has 4 walls. Each wall is 10 feet long. What is the perimeter of Diego's room?

Ⓐ 20 feet Ⓑ 40 feet Ⓒ 10 feet

4. Karen is half as tall as her older brother, Ben. Ben is 6 feet tall. How tall is Karen?

Ⓐ 5 feet tall Ⓑ 3 feet tall Ⓒ 2 feet tall

5. Susan's shelf can hold 2 pounds. Her dolls weigh 8 ounces each. How many dolls can Susan put on her shelf?

Ⓐ 2 dolls Ⓑ 4 dolls Ⓒ 6 dolls

Name ______________________ Date ____________

Problem Solving: Time and Money

Directions Darken the circle for the correct answer.

1. Josh had 82 dimes. He spent 24 dimes. How many dimes did he have left?

Ⓐ 106
Ⓑ 68
Ⓒ 58
Ⓓ 52

2. Kyle saved $5.00 to buy a present for his mother. The present he wants to buy costs $12.00. How much more money does Kyle need?

Ⓐ $17.00
Ⓑ $7.00
Ⓒ $2.00
Ⓓ $10.00

3. Jon earns $6 every week for taking out the trash. Last week he earned another $2 for cleaning the yard. How much money did he earn for the week?

Ⓐ $6 – $2 =
Ⓑ $6 + $2 =
Ⓒ $12 – $6 =
Ⓓ $12 – $2 =

4. What time is 5 hours after 1:00 P.M.?

Ⓐ 1:00 A.M.
Ⓑ 5:00 A.M.
Ⓒ 3:00 P.M.
Ⓓ 6:00 P.M.

5. Vera leaves home at 9:00 A.M. every day. It takes her 15 minutes to walk to school. Which clock shows the time she gets to school?

A

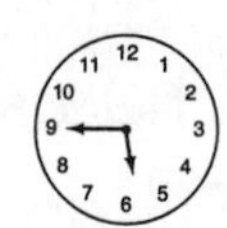
B

C

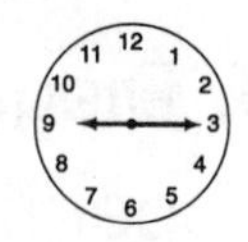
D

Ⓐ A
Ⓑ B
Ⓒ C
Ⓓ D

6. Dan set this alarm clock for 1 hour before he had to be at the dentist. What time did he have to be at the dentist?

Ⓐ 9:15
Ⓑ 12:15
Ⓒ 11:15
Ⓓ 11:00

Name ______________________ Date ____________

Science Overall Assessment

Directions Darken the circle for the correct answer.

1. _____ is a part of the water cycle.

Ⓐ Weather
Ⓑ Precipitation
Ⓒ Tornado

2. Solid water is called _____.

Ⓐ vapor
Ⓑ gas
Ⓒ ice

3. Earth's _____ is caused by temperature, clouds, and rain.

Ⓐ summer
Ⓑ weather
Ⓒ air

4. This storm happens in the winter.

Ⓐ hurricane
Ⓑ tornado
Ⓒ blizzard

5. This storm has a funnel.

Ⓐ hurricane
Ⓑ tornado
Ⓒ blizzard

6. Land is made of soil and _____.

Ⓐ rock
Ⓑ Sun
Ⓒ wind

7. The Sun gives light to the Earth and the _____.

Ⓐ Moon
Ⓑ Sun
Ⓒ stars

8. _____ is the largest planet.

Ⓐ Earth
Ⓑ Mars
Ⓒ Jupiter

9. Dogs are _____.

Ⓐ mammals
Ⓑ reptiles
Ⓒ amphibians

10. _____ does not take a lot of energy.

Ⓐ swimming
Ⓑ reading
Ⓒ skating

Name ______________________ Date ______________

Earth and Space Science

Directions Darken the circle for the correct answer.

1. Most of the Earth is covered by _____.

Ⓐ grass
Ⓑ woods
Ⓒ water

2. Air is an invisible _____.

Ⓐ solid
Ⓑ liquid
Ⓒ gas

3. _____ are hardened shapes of plants and animals.

Ⓐ Liquids
Ⓑ Fossils
Ⓒ Dinosaurs

4. The _____ revolves around the Earth.

Ⓐ Sun
Ⓑ Moon
Ⓒ North Pole

5. The _____ moves around the Sun.

Ⓐ shadow
Ⓑ Earth
Ⓒ wind

6. The planets orbit the _____.

Ⓐ Earth
Ⓑ Sun
Ⓒ Moon

7. Water changes _____.

Ⓐ rocks
Ⓑ wind
Ⓒ light

8. Rain comes from _____.

Ⓐ erosion
Ⓑ clouds
Ⓒ degrees

9. Clouds help us know what the _____ will be.

Ⓐ weather
Ⓑ erosion
Ⓒ degrees

10. Thermometers measure _____.

Ⓐ wind speed
Ⓑ temperature
Ⓒ water level

Name ______________________ Date ______________

Earth and Space Science, p. 2

Directions Answer each question in a complete sentence.

1. What are the three forms of matter?

____

____

2. What does the word **extinct** mean?

____

____

3. Name three of the planets in our solar system.

____

____

4. Name two forms of precipitation.

____

____

5. What are two types of dangerous storms?

____

____

Name ______________________ Date ____________

Life Science

Directions Darken the circle for the correct answer.

1. The natural home of a plant or an animal is called a ____.

Ⓐ forest
Ⓑ habitat
Ⓒ shelter

2. An ____ is everything around a living thing.

Ⓐ environment
Ⓑ animal
Ⓒ ocean

3. Plants and animals ____ with each other in their environments.

Ⓐ play
Ⓑ learn
Ⓒ interact

4. ____ grow into new plants.

Ⓐ Seeds
Ⓑ Needles
Ⓒ Stems

5. Roots get water from the ____.

Ⓐ air
Ⓑ soil
Ⓒ leaves

6. The ____ make food for the plants.

Ⓐ stems
Ⓑ roots
Ⓒ leaves

7. Lizards and snakes are ____.

Ⓐ mammals
Ⓑ reptiles
Ⓒ fish

8. Your body uses ____ to run, jump, and swim.

Ⓐ teeth
Ⓑ health
Ⓒ energy

9. Look both ways before you cross the ____.

Ⓐ street
Ⓑ room
Ⓒ stage

10. During a thunderstorm, you should ____.

Ⓐ go swimming
Ⓑ use a computer or phone
Ⓒ stay indoors

Name ______________________ Date ____________

Life Science, p. 2

Directions Answer each question in a complete sentence.

1. Tell three things that living things need.

2. Why do all living things need plants?

3. Name two of the things that plants need to make food.

4. How do scientists find out about animals that lived years ago?

5. Name four of the five senses.

Name ____________________ Date ____________

Physical Science

Directions Darken the circle for the correct answer.

1. We get most of our light from the ____.

Ⓐ Sun
Ⓑ Moon
Ⓒ lamp

2. Light moves in a ____ line.

Ⓐ dotted
Ⓑ wavy
Ⓒ straight

3. Light ____ off things we see.

Ⓐ blocks
Ⓑ reflects
Ⓒ lives

4. A whisper is a ____ sound.

Ⓐ loud
Ⓑ soft
Ⓒ deep

5. People make sound with their ____.

Ⓐ ears
Ⓑ eyes
Ⓒ throat

6. ____ have a shape.

Ⓐ Solids
Ⓑ Liquids
Ⓒ Gases

7. Water vapor is water in ____ form.

Ⓐ solid
Ⓑ liquid
Ⓒ gas

8. A ____ is a push or a pull.

Ⓐ force
Ⓑ direction
Ⓒ speed

9. Force can move things and change their ____.

Ⓐ color
Ⓑ shape
Ⓒ name

10. The force that pulls everything toward the ground is called ____.

Ⓐ gravity
Ⓑ weight
Ⓒ movement

Name ______________________ Date ______________

Physical Science, p. 2

Directions Answer each question in a complete sentence.

1. Name two sources of light.

____

____

2. Name something you could use to measure a solid.

____

____

3. Name something you could use to measure a liquid.

____

____

4. When does a liquid change to a gas?

____

____

5. Name three things that use wheels to move.

____

____

____

Name ______________________ Date ____________

Science Portfolio Assessment

Student's Name ______________________

Date ______________________

Goals	Evidence and Comments
1. Growth in understanding science concepts	
2. Growth in using science processes	
3. Growth in thinking critically	
4. Growth in developing positive habits of mind and positive attitudes toward science	

Name ______________________________ Date ______________

Social Studies Overall Assessment

Directions Darken the circle for the correct answer.

1. The first Americans were ____.

Ⓐ English people
Ⓑ American Indians
Ⓒ Pilgrims

2. American Indians got their clothing ____.

Ⓐ from stores
Ⓑ from the Pilgrims
Ⓒ by making it

3. Christopher Columbus sailed to America from ____.

Ⓐ Europe
Ⓑ China
Ⓒ South America

4. Money that people are paid for working is ____.

Ⓐ wants
Ⓑ goods
Ⓒ income

5. In the United States, people ____ for new leaders.

Ⓐ laws
Ⓑ governor
Ⓒ vote

6. Dirty air is one kind of ____.

Ⓐ pollution
Ⓑ community
Ⓒ service

7. The ____ is the leader of a state.

Ⓐ senator
Ⓑ governor
Ⓒ mayor

8. Canada is on the continent of ____.

Ⓐ Europe
Ⓑ North America
Ⓒ South America

9. A ____ shows the direction on a map.

Ⓐ compass rose
Ⓑ map key
Ⓒ equator

10. ____ can help a city grow.

Ⓐ Fires
Ⓑ Floods
Ⓒ Inventions

Name ______________________________ Date ______________

Social Studies Overall Assessment, p. 2

Directions

Darken the circle for correct answer.

1. The President of the United States is the leader of a _____.

Ⓐ city
Ⓑ state
Ⓒ country

2. The President of the United States lives in the _____.

Ⓐ Capitol
Ⓑ White House
Ⓒ Empire State Building

3. The _____ tells if a law is fair.

Ⓐ President
Ⓑ Supreme Court
Ⓒ Congress

4. A globe is a _____.

Ⓐ a model of the Earth
Ⓑ a photograph of the Earth
Ⓒ a graph of the Earth

5. _____ is part of culture.

Ⓐ Height
Ⓑ Language
Ⓒ Rain

Directions

Circle the word that goes best with each picture.

6. 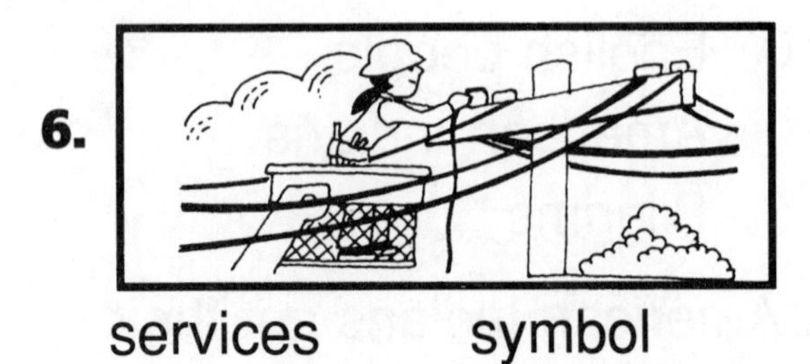

services symbol

7. 

goods services

8. 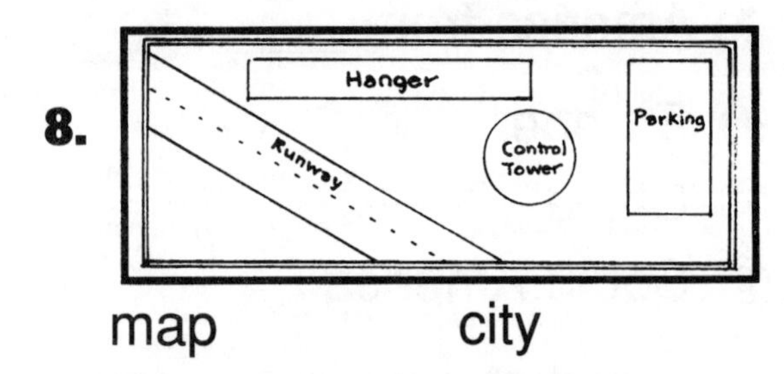

map city

9. 

law leader

10. 

community country

Name ______________________ Date ____________

Social Studies Overall Assessment, p. 3

Directions Answer each question in a complete sentence.

1. Why is water important to people?

____

____

2. List two things people do to help their community.

____

____

3. Why is it good to learn about other people's holidays?

____

____

4. Why is it smart to use money wisely?

____

____

____

5. Name two things your community spends tax money on.

____

____

Name ______________________________ Date ______________

Reading Maps

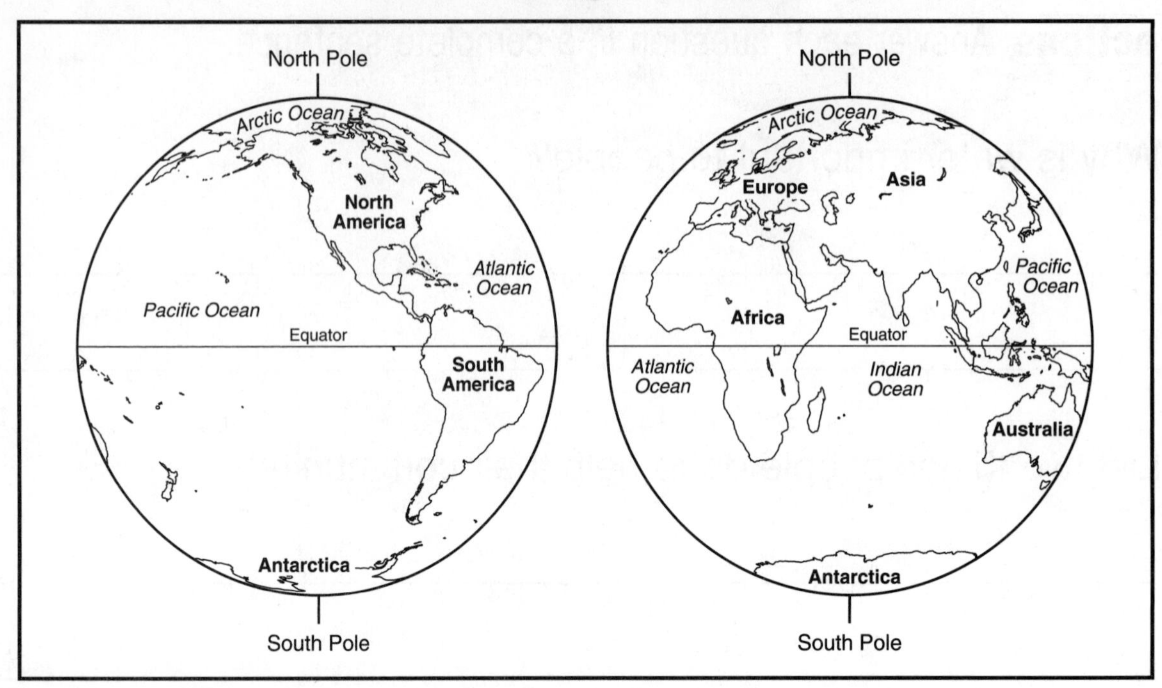

Directions Use the map to answer the questions.

1. On which continent is the South Pole?

____

2. Name three oceans. ______________________________

____

3. Is Australia closer to the North Pole or the South Pole?

____

4. Which ocean is between North America and Europe?

____

5. What is one continent that the equator passes through?

____

Name _______________________________ Date _______________

Reading Maps

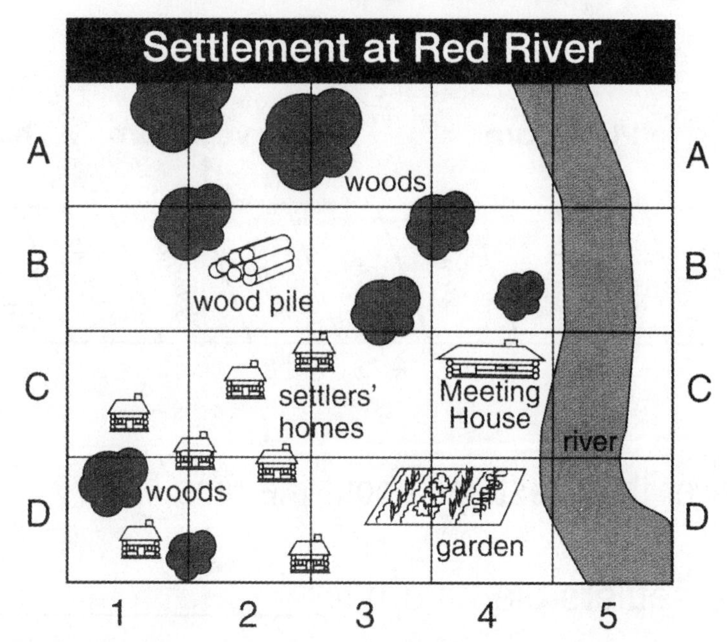

Directions Use the map grid to answer the questions. Darken the circle for the correct answer.

1. What is in B-2?

Ⓐ wood pile Ⓑ garden Ⓒ river

2. In which square is the Meeting House?

Ⓐ A-1 Ⓑ B-4 Ⓒ C-4

3. How many squares are between the river and the settlers' homes?

Ⓐ 3 Ⓑ 2 Ⓒ 0

4. What is in square A-3?

Ⓐ garden Ⓑ river Ⓒ woods

5. In which squares is the garden?

Ⓐ D-3 and D-4 Ⓑ C-2 and C-3 Ⓒ B-1 and C-1

Name ______________________ Date ____________

Using Time Lines and Charts

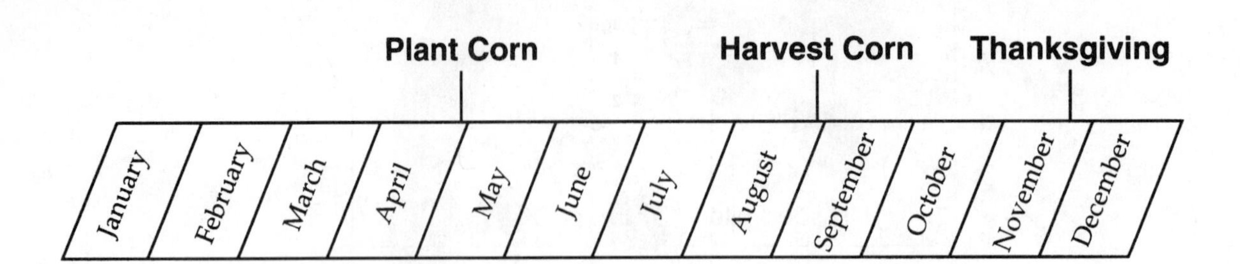

Directions Answer the questions about the time line.

1. When did the settlers plant corn? ____________

2. How many months did the corn take to grow?

____

3. What month comes after Thanksgiving? ____________

Large Rivers	
River	Continent
Amazon	South America
Hwang	Asia
Mississippi	North America
Nile	Africa
Rhine	Europe

Directions Use the table to answer the questions.

4. What is the Nile? ____________

5. Where is the Amazon? ____________

6. What river is in North America? ____________

Skills Assessments, Grade 2
Answer Key

Page 5

1. x
2. j
3. z
4. A
5. B
6. C
7. A
8. Students circle: stork, shark, horse, bird, lark.

Page 6

1. C
2. C
3. C
4. B
5. B

Page 7

1. w, g, n
2. k
3. k
4. q
5. h
6. s
7. p, p, r
8. b

Page 8

1. p
2. n
3. t
4. d
5. f
6. g
7. r
8. l

Page 9

1. A, pen; B, vest; C, ten
2. A, cat; C, lamp; D, van
3. A, drum; B, duck; D, rug
4. A, sock; C, blocks; D, frog
5. B, bib; C, pig; D, king

Page 10

1. A, queen; D, seal
2. B, jay; C, sail; D, game
3. B, tube; C, fuse
4. B, goat; C, hoe; D, robe
5. A, bike; C, pie; D, sky

Page 11

1. A
2. C
3. B
4. A
5. B
6. C
7. A
8. B

Page 12

1. A
2. A
3. B
4. A
5. A
6. A
7. A
8. B
9. A
10. A

Page 13

1. B
2. A
3. C
4. B
5. C
6. C
7. A
8. A

Page 14

Answers will vary according to teacher's choice of words.

Page 15

1. C
2. A
3. C
4. A
5. C
6. C
7. A
8. B
9. A
10. A

Page 16

1. D
2. C
3. B
4. A
5. D
6. D
7. B
8. C

Page 17

1. D
2. C
3. D
4. D
5. C

Page 18

1. C
2. D
3. C
4. D
5. B
6. B
7. C
8. D

Page 19

1. B
2. A
3. D
4. B
5. A
6. C
7. C
8. C

Page 20

Students circle:

1. van, jeep, bike
2. meat, cake, bun
3. horn, harp, chirp, purr
4. barn, horse, corn, dirt, herd
5. shorts, shirt, skirt

Page 21

1. D
2. A
3. C
4. D
5. C
6. B
7. A
8. D

Page 22

1. A
2. C
3. C
4. B
5. A

Page 23

1. A
2. A
3. C
4. B

Page 24

1. B
2. C
3. A
4. B

Page 25

1. A
2. C
3. B

Page 26

1. They went to the park and flew Jason's kite.
2. They took a nap.
3. Maria looked under the bed.
4. She found her doll in the buggy.

Page 27

1. C
2. B

Page 28

1. I saw many flags in my neighborhood.
2. Annie likes to play basketball.
3. Bill has lots of friends.

Page 29

1. A
2. B
3. B

Page 30

1. The Hole
2. small boy, mice
3. The boy falls down a hole.
4. The mice show the boy a way out.

Page 32

1. C
2. B
3. A
4. C
5. A

Page 34

1. The soil was worn out, so the cotton would not grow.
2. She used the cotton to make clothes to sell.
3. The worm was stuck on a wire.
4. The girl and the worms lived happily ever after.
5. The worms made the soil rich.

Page 36

1. B
2. C
3. B
4. C
5. D

Page 38

1. The boy hears a noise from the attic.
2. He wants to find out about the noise.
3. The dog hid under a chair.
4. The boy discovered a squirrel.
5. The squirrel went across the street.

Page 40

1. A
2. B
3. C
4. B
5. B
6. A

Page 42

1. Trees need soil, water, and sunlight.
2. The roots take water from the soil.
3. Trees have bark for protection.
4. Trees give us shade and help keep the air clean.
5. Water moves up the trunk to the branches and leaves.

Page 43

1. A
2. B
3. A
4. A
5. B
6. C
7. B
8. B

Page 44

1. B
2. D
3. A
4. C
5. B
6. A
7. C
8. D

Page 45

1. C
2. A
3. B
4. B
5. C
6. C
7. A
8. B

Page 46

1. C
2. A
3. C
4. B
5. A
6. C
7. B
8. D

Page 47

1. house, thing
2. Alaska, place
3. hat, thing
4. shoe, thing
5. boy, person
6. B
7. C
8. C
9. B
10. A

Page 48

1. C
2. A
3. A
4. B
5. C
6. A
7. C
8. D

Page 49

1. D
2. C
3. D
4. B
5. A
6. C

Page 50

1. A
2. C
3. A
4. C
5. B
6. A
7. B
8. A
9. B
10. B

Page 51

1. B
2. C
3. B
4. D
5. B
6. C
7. B
8. D

Page 52

1. A
2. A
3. C
4. A
5. B
6. A
7. B
8. B
9. B
10. A

Page 54

1. D
2. C
3. B
4. B
5. C
6. A

Page 55

1. Florida
2. photographs
3. The World of Sharks
4. Deb Homan

Page 56

1. C
2. D
3. B
4. A

Page 57

1. hiking
2. canoeing
3. flying
4. tennis
5. skiing
6. skating
7. baby, barn, basket
8. happy, hat, hay
9. call, cart, cat
10. chain, chicken, chore

Page 58

1. race/run
2. bat/boy
3. see/sit
4. race/run
5. fit/fun
6. see/sit
7. this day
8. tiny
9. no
10. toad
11. toad
12. tiny/total

Page 59

1. Saturday is the best day of the week.
2. Answers will vary. Any of the other sentences in the paragraph contain details.
3. 3, 2, 4, 1

Page 60

1. My, I, We
2. First, then, after, or last
3. Answers will vary.

Answer Key, p. 2

Page 61

1. I just love a parade.
2. The uniforms shine with brass buttons and gold braid.
3. Answers will vary.
4. loud

Page 62

1. Sewing on a button can be easy.
2. Get a needle and thread.
3. needle, thread, button, and a piece of clothing
4. Answers will vary.

Page 63

1. to thank her grandmother
2. Grandma
3. October 22, 2000
4. The sweater fits, or the sweater is warm.

Page 64

1. D
2. B
3. B
4. C
5. B
6. C
7. A
8. C
9. C
10. D

Page 65

1. 82
2. 62
3. 59
4. 86
5. >
6. <
7. <
8. 65
9. 99
10. 29
11. 12:30
12. 5:00
13. 4:30
14. 693
15. 376
16. 710

Page 66

1. B
2. D
3. C
4. C
5. D
6. A

Page 67

1. C
2. B
3. B
4. C
5. C
6. B

Page 68

1. A
2. B
3. C
4. C
5. C
6. B
7. B
8. C

Page 69

1. B
2. B
3. C
4. C
5. A
6. B
7. C
8. C

Page 70

1. 18
2. 7
3. 23
4. 8
5. 8
6. 13
7. 74
8. 51
9. 65
10. 34
11. 84
12. 71

Page 71

1. A
2. C
3. B
4. C
5. C
6. B
7. B
8. C

Page 72

1. B
2. C
3. A
4. A
5. D
6. A
7. B
8. C

Page 73

1. 93, 89, 88, 85, 75
2. 34, **31**, **28**, **25**, 22, **19**, **16**, 13, **10**, **7**, **4**, 1
3. B
4. C
5. C
6. D

Page 74

1. 25¢, 30¢, 35¢, 36¢, 37¢, 37¢
2. 25¢, 50¢, 50¢
3. 50¢, 51¢, 51¢
4. 10¢, 20¢, 30¢, 40¢, 45¢, 46¢, 46¢
5. A
6. A

Page 75

1. 11:30
2. 5:30
3. 6:00
4. 9:15
5. 3:45
6. 7:30
7. B
8. C
9. B
10. A

Page 76

1. about 10 minutes
2. about 1 hour
3. <400
4. >500
5. A
6. C

Page 77

1. A
2. B
3. C
4. B
5. C
6. B

Page 78

1. D
2. C
3. C
4. C
5. B
6. A

Page 79

1. A
2. C
3. B
4. B
5. B

Page 80

1. C
2. B
3. B
4. D
5. D
6. C

Page 81

1. B
2. C
3. B
4. C
5. B
6. A
7. A
8. C
9. A
10. B

Page 82

1. C
2. C
3. B
4. B
5. B
6. B
7. A
8. B
9. A
10. B

Page 83

1. The three forms of matter are solids, liquids, and gases.
2. Answers will vary. The word **extinct** means that it doesn't exist now and there will never be any more of it.
3. Answers will vary. Students should name three planets from the following: Mercury, Venus, Earth, Mars, Jupiter, Saturn, Neptune, Uranus, and Pluto.

Page 83 cont....

4. Answers will vary. Students should name two of the following: rain, snow, sleet or hail.
5. Answers will vary. Students should name two from the following: blizzards, tornadoes, and hurricanes.

Page 84

1. B
2. A
3. C
4. A
5. B
6. C
7. B
8. C
9. A
10. C

Page 85

Answers will vary.

1. Living things need food, water, air, and shelter. Students name 3.
2. Plants produce oxygen, and they are food for plant eaters, which are the food for meat eaters.
3. Plants need sunlight, air, and water to make food. Students name 2 needs.
4. Scientists find out about animals that lived years ago by finding and studying fossils.
5. The five senses are sight, smell, hearing, taste, and touch. Students should name 4.

Page 86

1. A
2. C
3. B
4. B
5. C
6. A
7. C
8. A
9. B
10. A

Page 87

Answers will vary.

1. Sources of light are the Sun, stars, fireflies, candles, fire, light bulbs, and flashlights. Students should name 2 sources.
2. Something you could use to measure a solid is a ruler, tape measure, or yardstick. Students should name 1.
3. You could use a measuring cup to measure a liquid. Answers may vary.
4. A liquid changes to a gas when it reaches its boiling point or when it evaporates.
5. Things that use wheels to move are cars, trucks, wagons, baby carriages, trailers, pull toys, lawn mowers, bicycles, and tractors. Students should name 3.

Page 89

1. B
2. C
3. A
4. C
5. C
6. A
7. B
8. B
9. A
10. C

Page 90

1. C
2. B
3. B
4. A
5. B

Students circle:

6. services
7. goods
8. map
9. law
10. community

Page 91

Answers will vary.

1. People need water for drinking, washing things, and swimming. They cannot live without it.
2. Things people do to help their community are vote, get along with others, help make communities look beautiful, serve on committees, volunteer, or help others. Students name 2.
3. It is good to learn about other people's holidays so that we find out about their customs and beliefs that will help us to understand them.
4. It is smart to use money wisely because you can't buy everything at once; if you save some money, you'll have money to spend at another time or for emergencies.
5. Communities spend tax money on buses, parks, swimming pools, streets, police, fire departments, and emergency services. Students should name 2.

Page 92

1. Antarctica
2. Pacific, Atlantic, Indian, Arctic (Students name 3.)
3. South Pole
4. Atlantic
5. South America or Africa

Page 93

1. A
2. C
3. B
4. C
5. A

Page 94

1. April
2. 4
3. December
4. a river
5. South America
6. Mississippi